Print Your Own Money

Empowering Individuals in the Blockchain, Cryptocurrency & Web3 Era

SHAILENDRA KUMAR

Copyright Disclaimer: All information and events depicted in this book are based on publicly available information and sources. The characters and events are portrayed to the best of the author's ability using research from credible and accessible resources. The author and publisher have taken great care to ensure the accuracy of the information presented, but they do not assume any liability for any errors or omissions.

Dedicated to

My father Late Sri Ram Chandra Singh and mother Late Shanti Devi.

Preface

Imagine a world where you don't need banks to control your money or companies to own your data. A world where anyone, anywhere, can create their own currency, design their own financial system and have full control over their economic future. That's the promise of blockchain, cryptocurrency and Web3.

This book, *Print Your Own Money: Empowering Individuals in the Blockchain, Cryptocurrency & Web3 Era*, is about how this new technology is changing everything. It's not just for tech experts or financial wizards. It's for everyone. Whether you're an artist, a small business owner, a community leader or just curious about what's next, this book will help you understand how Web3 can give you the power to take charge of your own economic destiny.

For centuries, money and finance have been controlled by governments and large institutions. But with blockchain technology, we now have tools to create personal and community-driven currencies. These tools are open to anyone with an internet connection. They are designed to give people more freedom, transparency and fairness.

In this book, you'll learn:

- How money has evolved and why blockchain is the next big step.
- What cryptocurrencies like Bitcoin and Ethereum are and why they matter.
- How individuals and communities are already creating their own tokens.
- The challenges and risks of this new financial system.
- The exciting future of personal currencies in the digital age.

This is not a book filled with technical jargon. It's written in simple, clear language for everyone to understand. You'll see real-world examples and step-by-step guides to explore how Web3 works and how you can get started.

The power to print your own money is no longer a dream. It's a reality made possible by blockchain and Web3. This book is your guide to understanding this incredible shift and finding your place in it.

Welcome to the future of money. Let's build it together.

Shailendra Kumar

Acknowledgments

Writing this book has been an incredible journey and I owe a great deal of gratitude to the people and communities who inspired and supported me along the way.

First and foremost, I want to thank the blockchain pioneers, visionaries and developers who built the foundation of this transformative technology. Without their courage to question the status quo and their relentless innovation, this book - and the ideas within it - would not exist.

I am deeply grateful to the vibrant Web3 community. From forums and hackathons to DAOs and social media discussions, your passion and collaboration have fueled my understanding of this space. The real-world examples and stories in this book are a reflection of your efforts and creativity.

To my friends and colleagues who shared their knowledge, provided feedback and encouraged me to think deeper - thank you. Your insights helped shape this book into what it is today.

To my readers, this book is for you. Whether you are new to blockchain or already building your place in the Web3 world, your curiosity and enthusiasm are what drive this movement forward.

Finally, I want to acknowledge the power of the technology itself. Blockchain, cryptocurrency and Web3 represent not just tools, but a profound shift in how we think about money, ownership and empowerment. It is my hope that this book helps you unlock its potential in your own life.

Here's to a future where everyone has the power to create, connect and thrive. Thank you for joining me on this journey.

With gratitude,

Shailendra Kumar

Index

Introduction 1
    The Age of Digital Sovereignty 2
        Brief History of Money and Its Centralization 2
        How Blockchain Redefines Individual Empowerment 5
    Web3: The Internet of Value 9
        Overview of Web3 and Decentralized Infrastructure 9
        Evolution from Web1 to Web3 13
Part I: The Building Blocks 19
    Blockchain: The Technology of Trust 20
        Fundamentals of Blockchain 20
        Key Attributes of Blockchain: Decentralization, Immutability, Transparency 25
    Cryptocurrency: More than Digital Cash 30
        Origins of Bitcoin and the Idea of Digital Scarcity 30
        Evolution into Smart Contracts and Programmable Money . 35
    Tokenomics: The New Economics of Digital Assets 41
        Types of Tokens: Utility, Governance, Social Tokens, NFTs 41
        Basics of Token Design and Value Creation 47
Part II: Printing Your Own Currency 54
    What Does "Printing Your Currency" Mean in Web3? 55
        From Central Banks to Personal Tokenization 55
        Examples: Creators, Communities and DAOs Launching Tokens 60
    Designing a Personal or Community Token 65
        Purpose: Why Launch a Token? 65
        Key Considerations: Supply, Utility and Governance 70
    Tools and Platforms 76
        Overview of Tools Like Ethereum, Solana, Binance Smart Chain and Layer 2 Solutions 76
        No-Code Options for Launching Tokens 82
Part III: Use Cases and Real-World Examples 87
    Creator Economies: Empowering Artists and Influencers 88
        Case Studies: Social Tokens and NFTs 88
    Community Economies 94
        DAOs and Shared Value Systems 94
        Local and Global Initiatives 99
    Financial Inclusion through Web3 105

Impact on Unbanked and Underbanked Populations........ 105
Part IV: Challenges and Risks..**111**
    Regulatory Hurdles.. 112
        Navigating the Legal Landscape..112
        Balancing Innovation and Compliance...............................118
    Security and Scalability Concerns.. 125
        Risks in Smart Contracts and Tokenomics........................ 125
        Solutions Like Auditing and Layer 2 Tech..........................131
    Market Risks and Adoption Barriers.. 137
        Speculation vs. Utility..137
        Overcoming Adoption Challenges..................................... 142
Part V: The Future of Personal Currencies...................................**148**
    Interoperability and the Metaverse... 149
        How Personal Currencies Fit into a Connected, Immersive Future.. 149
    AI and Personalized Finance.. 155
        Role of AI in Managing and Optimizing Personal Currencies.. 155
    Redefining Global Economics...162
        Vision for Decentralized and Community-Driven Financial Systems... 162
Appendices..**168**
    Empowering the Individual in the Digital Age: A Recap.............169
    Glossary of Terms...171
    Resources for Learning Blockchain and Web3.........................179
    Guide to Token Launch Tools and Platforms............................ 184

Introduction

The Age of Digital Sovereignty

Brief History of Money and Its Centralization

Money has always been an essential part of human life. It allows people to trade goods and services. But how money works has changed a lot over time. Let's explore how it started and how it became centralized.

Barter System
In the earliest times, people didn't have money. They traded goods directly. For example, if you had apples and wanted rice, you'd find someone who had rice and wanted apples. This was called the barter system. It worked but had problems. What if the other person didn't want your apples? Or what if you couldn't agree on how many apples equal a bag of rice?

Commodity Money
To solve this, people started using things everyone agreed had value, like gold, silver or salt. These were called commodity money. For example:

- In ancient Africa, salt was so valuable it was used as money.
- In the Roman Empire, soldiers were often paid in salt (which is where the word "salary" comes from!).

But carrying gold or salt was heavy and inconvenient. So, societies found a new way.

Paper Money
People began trusting central authorities, like kings or governments, to issue money. This money didn't have value on its own, but people believed in its value because the authority said so. For instance:

- In China, around 1000 AD, the first paper money was introduced. The government promised it could be exchanged for gold or goods.
- In the 1700s, modern banking systems in Europe started issuing paper notes backed by gold.

Centralized Money and Banks
Over time, governments and banks took full control of money. This system is called **centralized finance**. They print money, decide its value and control its flow.

Example: In the U.S., the Federal Reserve (the central bank) manages the dollar. It decides how much money to print and sets rules for its use.

This system works well for many, but it also creates problems.

- If a government prints too much money, it can cause inflation, where money loses value.
- Centralized systems can exclude people. For example, over a billion people worldwide don't have access to banks.

The Rise of Digital Money
As technology improved, we moved to digital money. Today, most money exists in bank accounts or as numbers on a

screen. You don't see physical money when you use credit cards or mobile apps like PayPal or Venmo.

But digital money is still controlled by banks and governments. If your bank blocks your account, you lose access to your money. This is where blockchain and cryptocurrency bring a big change.

How Blockchain Redefines Individual Empowerment

Blockchain is a revolutionary technology that changes how we think about trust, ownership and money. It gives power back to individuals, letting them control their assets and decisions without relying on middlemen like banks or governments.

Blockchain
At its core, blockchain is a digital ledger - a record book that anyone can access but no one can alter without agreement from others.

- Every transaction is stored in blocks.
- These blocks are linked together to form a chain, making the data secure and transparent.

For example, if Alice sends money to Bob using a blockchain network like Bitcoin, the transaction is permanently recorded. No one can delete or modify it.

Removing the Middlemen
Traditionally, banks and financial institutions act as middlemen for most transactions. They keep records, verify payments and charge fees. Blockchain eliminates the need for these intermediaries.

Example: If you send money abroad using a bank, it may take days, with high fees. Using blockchain, you can transfer cryptocurrency directly to someone anywhere in the world within minutes, often at a fraction of the cost.

This gives people full control over their money and reduces dependence on centralized systems.

Ownership and Control

Blockchain introduces the idea of **self-custody**, where you own your assets directly without relying on third parties.

- With traditional banks, your money is technically under their control. If they freeze your account, you lose access.
- On blockchain, you store your cryptocurrency in a digital wallet that only you can access using a private key (a secret password).

Example:

- Imagine your government limits how much money you can withdraw during a crisis. With cryptocurrency, no one can stop you from using your funds.

Decentralization and Freedom

Blockchain is decentralized, meaning no single entity controls it. Instead, it's run by a network of computers worldwide. This ensures fairness and transparency.

Example: Platforms like Ethereum allow anyone to create decentralized applications (dApps) without asking for permission from a central authority.

This opens doors for creators, businesses and individuals to operate freely and securely.

Financial Inclusion
Blockchain empowers people who are excluded from traditional financial systems.

- Over 1.4 billion people globally don't have access to banks, especially in developing countries. Blockchain provides them with tools to store, send and receive money using just a smartphone and an internet connection.

Example:

- In countries like Venezuela, where hyperinflation has destroyed the value of local currency, people use cryptocurrencies like Bitcoin to preserve their wealth and make transactions.

Empowering Creators and Communities
Blockchain also redefines how creators and communities interact with their audiences.

- Artists can sell digital art as NFTs (non-fungible tokens) and earn directly from their work without paying middlemen.
- Communities can launch their own tokens to fund projects and share value.

Example:

- A musician can release their album as an NFT, giving fans direct access while keeping all profits.

Immutable Records and Trust
Blockchain creates a world where everyone can trust the system without needing to trust each other.

- Transactions are permanent and transparent, reducing fraud.
- Smart contracts (self-executing agreements) ensure fairness.

Example:

- Imagine hiring a freelancer. You both agree on terms using a smart contract. The contract automatically releases payment once the job is done, eliminating disputes.

The Power of Self-Sovereignty
At its heart, blockchain empowers individuals to:

- Control their money without intermediaries.
- Own their data and digital identity.
- Participate in a global economy on equal terms.

This shift is what we call **digital sovereignty** - the freedom to manage your financial and digital life without outside control.

Web3: The Internet of Value

Overview of Web3 and Decentralized Infrastructure

Web3 is the next generation of the internet. Unlike the current internet (Web2), where companies like Google, Facebook and Amazon control most of the data and services, Web3 is about **decentralization** - giving power back to the people.

Let's understand what Web3 is, how it works and why it matters.

What Is Web3?

Web3 is often called the **"Internet of Value"** because it allows people to exchange value (like money, assets or services) directly, without relying on big companies or banks.

- Web1 (1990s): The "read-only" internet. People could only view static web pages.
- Web2 (2000s): The "read-write" internet. Social media and platforms let people create and share content, but companies owned the data.
- Web3 (now): The "read-write-own" internet. People can own their data, money and digital identity.

Example:

- In Web2, if you sell a digital item in a game like Fortnite, the company owns the marketplace and can take a cut or delete your account.
- In Web3, you can sell the same item as an NFT on a blockchain, keeping full control and ownership.

9

How Does Web3 Work?

Web3 relies on **decentralized infrastructure** powered by blockchain and related technologies.

- **Blockchain**: Stores data in a secure, tamper-proof way.
- **Smart Contracts**: Automated agreements that execute without intermediaries.
- **Decentralized Applications (dApps)**: Apps that run on blockchain networks instead of centralized servers.

Example:

- Instead of using Uber (a centralized company), you could use a dApp to connect directly with drivers, paying them directly without Uber taking a commission.

Decentralized Infrastructure: Key Components

- **Cryptocurrencies**: The currency of Web3. They allow peer-to-peer transactions without banks.

Example: Bitcoin for payments or Ethereum for dApps.

- **Decentralized Finance (DeFi)**: Financial services without banks.

Example: Borrowing money on platforms like Aave, where people lend and borrow directly.

- **Decentralized Storage**: Replacing centralized servers (like Google Drive) with systems like IPFS (InterPlanetary File System).

Example: Storing your files on IPFS means no one can block or delete them.

- **Decentralized Autonomous Organizations (DAOs)**: Groups that run projects without centralized leadership.

Example: A DAO could manage a community fund, where members vote on how to spend money.

Why Web3 Matters

- **Ownership of Data**: In Web3, you own your data.

Example: Instead of Facebook profiting from your photos and posts, you could earn rewards for sharing your content.

- **Borderless Economy**: Web3 connects people globally without restrictions.

Example: A freelancer in Kenya can get paid directly in cryptocurrency, avoiding high international transfer fees.

- **Trustless Systems**: Web3 replaces trust in companies with trust in code.

Example: Instead of trusting a bank to process your loan, a smart contract ensures fairness automatically.

Real-World Applications of Web3

- **Finance**: DeFi apps like Uniswap let people trade cryptocurrencies directly, without middlemen.

- **Gaming**: Games like Axie Infinity allow players to earn real money by playing.
- **Social Media**: Platforms like Lens Protocol let users own their posts and profiles.
- **Identity**: Web3 wallets like MetaMask give users a secure, portable identity.

Challenges of Web3

While Web3 offers many benefits, it's still evolving.

- Learning curve: People need to understand how wallets, private keys and dApps work.
- Scalability: Blockchain networks need to handle more users efficiently.
- Regulation: Governments are still figuring out how to regulate decentralized systems.

Web3 is not just a new technology; it's a movement to create a fairer, more inclusive internet. It puts power in the hands of individuals, allowing them to control their money, data and interactions.

Evolution from Web1 to Web3

The internet has come a long way since its creation. Each phase of its evolution - Web1, Web2 and now Web3 - represents a step toward more interaction, creativity and personal empowerment. Let's break down this journey.

Web1: The "Read-Only" Era (1990s – early 2000s)

Web1 was the very first version of the internet. It was like a giant library where people could only read information. There was no way to interact or create your own content easily.

Key Features of Web1:

- **Static Websites:** Websites were simple and looked like digital brochures.

Example: A travel website in Web1 might only display flight schedules, but you couldn't book a ticket online.

- **One-Way Communication:** Companies or organizations published content and users could only consume it.

Example: News websites posted articles, but readers couldn't comment or share opinions.

- **No Personalization:** Everyone saw the same content, regardless of preferences.

Example of Web1 Websites:

- Yahoo! in its early days.
- Britannica Online for digital encyclopedias.

Web2: The "Read-Write" Era (2000s – Present)

Web2 introduced the internet we're most familiar with today. It allowed people not only to consume content but also to create and share their own. This shift led to the rise of social media, e-commerce and user-generated platforms.

Key Features of Web2:

- **Interactive and Dynamic Websites:** Users could log in, personalize their experience and interact with content.

Example: Amazon recommends products based on your browsing history.

- **Social Media:** Platforms like Facebook, Instagram and YouTube let users share posts, videos and photos.

Example: A single tweet or video could go viral, reaching millions.

- **Centralized Platforms:** Large companies like Google, Facebook and Amazon became gatekeepers of the internet. They owned the servers, controlled the data and profited from user activity.

Benefits of Web2:

- Easy to use and highly interactive.
- Millions of people gained access to information, commerce and social connections.

Drawbacks of Web2:

....

- **Lack of Ownership:** Users created content, but companies owned it. For instance, if Instagram shuts down your account, you lose all your photos and followers.
- **Data Exploitation:** Platforms collected user data to sell ads and make profits, often without clear consent.

Example: Facebook's data scandals revealed how user information was misused.

Web3: The "Read-Write-Own" Era (Now and Beyond)

Web3 is a new version of the internet that addresses the problems of Web2. It allows users to own their data, content and digital identity while interacting directly without relying on centralized platforms.

Key Features of Web3:

- **Decentralization:** No single company or organization controls the system. Instead, it runs on blockchain technology.

Example: Instead of storing your videos on YouTube's servers, you could use a decentralized platform like Livepeer, where no one can delete your content.

- **User Ownership:** Users own their data and assets through wallets, tokens and NFTs.

Example: On Web3 social media platforms like Lens Protocol, your profile belongs to you, not the platform.

- **Direct Transactions:** People can trade, collaborate or interact without intermediaries.

Example: Artists selling digital art as NFTs directly to fans, without paying fees to platforms like Etsy or eBay.

Comparing the Evolution of the Internet

Aspect	Web1	Web2	Web3
User Role	Reader	Creator	Owner
Control	Centralized by websites	Centralized by platforms	Decentralized via blockchain
Content	Static	Dynamic and interactive	Owned by users
Data Ownership	No ownership	Owned by platforms	Owned by individuals
Examples	Yahoo!, Britannica	Facebook, YouTube, Amazon	Ethereum, NFTs, DAOs

Why Web3 Is Important

- **Empowers Individuals:** Users have full control over their data, money and identity.
- **Fairer Economy:** Creators and users share the value they generate instead of giving it all to platforms.

- **Global Accessibility:** Web3 works for anyone with an internet connection, removing barriers like censorship or banking restrictions.

Web3 is not just an upgrade to the internet; it's a complete transformation. It represents a future where individuals - not corporations - are at the center. In the next section, we'll explore how cryptocurrencies are the backbone of this decentralized web and how they enable a fairer, freer digital world.

Part I: The Building Blocks

Blockchain: The Technology of Trust

Fundamentals of Blockchain

Blockchain is the foundation of Web3. It is a revolutionary technology that ensures trust, transparency and security without needing a central authority. But what exactly is blockchain and how does it work? Let's break it down.

What Is Blockchain?

At its core, a blockchain is a **digital ledger** that records transactions. Unlike traditional ledgers kept by banks or governments, a blockchain is decentralized, meaning no single entity controls it.

Key Features:

- **Decentralized:** No central authority. Everyone on the network has a copy of the data.
- **Immutable:** Once data is recorded, it cannot be changed.
- **Transparent:** All transactions are visible to everyone on the network.

How Does Blockchain Work?

Blockchain operates in a series of steps:

1. **Transactions Are Initiated:**
    - Example: Alice wants to send 1 Bitcoin to Bob.

- She creates a transaction request using her digital wallet.
2. **Transaction Is Verified:**
   - The blockchain network verifies Alice has enough Bitcoin to send.
   - This process uses **nodes** (computers in the network) to check the transaction's validity.
3. **Transaction Is Added to a Block:**
   - Once verified, the transaction is grouped with others into a "block."
4. **Consensus Is Achieved:**
   - Nodes agree on the block's validity through a process called **consensus** (e.g., Proof of Work or Proof of Stake).
   - This ensures no fraudulent transactions are added.
5. **Block Is Added to the Chain:**
   - The new block is linked to the previous block, forming a continuous, unbreakable chain of records.
6. **Transaction Is Finalized:**
   - Bob receives the 1 Bitcoin and the transaction is permanently recorded.

Key Components of Blockchain

- **Blocks:** Containers that store data, including transactions, timestamps and a unique identifier called a hash.
- **Chains:** Blocks are linked together, creating a secure and chronological history.
- **Nodes:** Computers that maintain the network by storing a copy of the blockchain and validating transactions.

- **Consensus Mechanisms:** Algorithms that ensure everyone in the network agrees on the validity of transactions.
    - **Proof of Work (PoW):** Used by Bitcoin; requires solving complex puzzles.
    - **Proof of Stake (PoS):** Used by Ethereum; validators are chosen based on the amount of cryptocurrency they hold and stake.

Why Is Blockchain Called the "Technology of Trust"?

Blockchain removes the need for trust in intermediaries like banks or governments. Instead, it relies on math, cryptography and transparency.

Example:

- In traditional banking, you trust the bank to send your money. If the bank fails, you lose access.
- On blockchain, the system itself ensures the transaction happens securely, with no need for a middleman.

Real-World Applications of Blockchain

- **Cryptocurrency:** Bitcoin and Ethereum enable peer-to-peer transactions without banks.
- **Supply Chain Management:** Companies like Walmart use blockchain to track food from farms to stores, ensuring safety and transparency.
- **Digital Identity:** Blockchain allows individuals to own and control their digital identities.

Example: Instead of signing in with Facebook, you could use a blockchain wallet to prove your identity.

- **Voting Systems:** Blockchain ensures secure, transparent and tamper-proof elections.

Advantages of Blockchain

- **Security:** Transactions are encrypted and protected against fraud.
- **Transparency:** Everyone can see the data, but sensitive information is anonymized.
- **Efficiency:** Transactions are faster and cheaper than traditional systems.
- **Global Access:** Anyone with an internet connection can use blockchain technology.

Challenges of Blockchain

While blockchain is powerful, it's not perfect.

- **Scalability:** Popular blockchains like Bitcoin can process only a limited number of transactions per second.
- **Energy Consumption:** Proof of Work systems require large amounts of energy.
- **Complexity:** Many people find blockchain hard to understand and use.

Blockchain is more than just a technology; it's a new way of thinking about trust, ownership and value. In the next chapter, we'll explore how cryptocurrencies leverage blockchain to empower individuals and reshape the global economy.

Key Attributes of Blockchain: Decentralization, Immutability, Transparency

Blockchain is a powerful technology because of its core attributes: **decentralization, immutability** and **transparency**. These features set blockchain apart from traditional systems and make it the foundation of Web3.

Decentralization: Power Without Central Control

In traditional systems, a central authority - like a bank, government or big tech company - controls data and transactions. Blockchain removes this central control by distributing the system across a network of computers (nodes).

How It Works:

- Each node stores a complete copy of the blockchain.
- Decisions, such as adding a new block, are made collectively through **consensus mechanisms** (e.g., Proof of Work or Proof of Stake).

Benefits of Decentralization:

- **No Single Point of Failure:** Unlike a centralized system that can be hacked or shut down, blockchain continues to work as long as some nodes are active.

Example: In 2016, a major centralized internet service provider went offline due to a cyberattack. A decentralized network like Bitcoin is immune to such attacks.

- **Freedom from Censorship:** No single entity can block or alter transactions.

Example: In authoritarian countries, individuals have used Bitcoin to transfer money without fear of government interference.

Real-World Analogy:
Think of decentralization like a village market. Everyone trades directly with one another, without needing a market manager to oversee every transaction.

Immutability: Records That Can't Be Altered

Immutability means that once data is added to the blockchain, it cannot be changed or deleted.

How It Works:

- Each block contains a unique **hash** (a cryptographic code) that links it to the previous block.
- Changing even a single transaction in one block would require altering all subsequent blocks - a nearly impossible task because it would need the approval of the entire network.

Benefits of Immutability:

- **Prevents Fraud:** No one can alter or delete records to cover up wrongdoing.

Example: In traditional accounting, records can be falsified. On blockchain, every transaction is permanent and verifiable.

- **Trustworthy Records:** Blockchain creates a reliable history of transactions.

Example: Walmart uses blockchain to track the supply chain of food products, ensuring the data can't be tampered with.

Real-World Analogy:
Imagine writing in permanent ink in a book. Once written, the words can't be erased or edited. That's how blockchain works.

Transparency: Everyone Can See What's Happening

Transparency means that all transactions on the blockchain are visible to every participant in the network.

How It Works:

- Transactions are stored on a public ledger that anyone can access.
- While transactions are visible, blockchain uses cryptography to protect user identities, showing only wallet addresses, not personal information.

Benefits of Transparency:

- **Accountability:** All actions are recorded and open to scrutiny.

Example: Governments and NGOs can use blockchain to show how funds are spent, ensuring donations reach their intended purpose.

- **Reduces Corruption:** Transparency discourages dishonest behavior.

Example: In land registry systems, blockchain can prevent fake ownership claims by making all property records publicly verifiable.

Real-World Analogy:
Think of a glass safe. Everyone can see what's inside, but only the person with the key can access it.

Why These Attributes Matter Together

When combined, decentralization, immutability and transparency create a system that is:

- **Secure:** Decentralization makes it resistant to hacking and censorship.
- **Trustworthy:** Immutability ensures data is reliable and unchangeable.
- **Fair:** Transparency holds everyone accountable and prevents misuse of power.

Example of All Three in Action:
Bitcoin, the first blockchain, embodies these attributes:

- **Decentralized:** No single person or institution controls Bitcoin.
- **Immutable:** Every Bitcoin transaction since 2009 is permanently recorded.
- **Transparent:** Anyone can view the entire transaction history on the blockchain.

Blockchain's key attributes are why it's called the "technology of trust." They enable systems that are fairer, more secure and more efficient than traditional centralized systems.

In the next section, we'll explore how consensus mechanisms like Proof of Work and Proof of Stake ensure trust and security in decentralized networks.

Cryptocurrency: More than Digital Cash

Origins of Bitcoin and the Idea of Digital Scarcity

Cryptocurrency began with a groundbreaking idea: creating money that exists only in the digital world, free from banks or governments. At the heart of this innovation is **Bitcoin**, the first cryptocurrency and the concept of **digital scarcity**, which gives it value.

The Birth of Bitcoin

In 2008, during a global financial crisis, an anonymous individual or group called **Satoshi Nakamoto** released a whitepaper titled *"Bitcoin: A Peer-to-Peer Electronic Cash System."* This document proposed a new type of money that didn't rely on banks or intermediaries.

Key Features of Bitcoin:

- **Decentralized:** No central authority controls Bitcoin. It operates on a blockchain network maintained by users.
- **Limited Supply:** Bitcoin has a fixed supply of 21 million coins, ensuring scarcity.
- **Peer-to-Peer Transactions:** People can send Bitcoin directly to each other without needing banks or payment processors.

The First Bitcoin Transaction:

- In 2009, Satoshi Nakamoto mined the first Bitcoin block, known as the **Genesis Block**.

- In 2010, the first real-world transaction occurred: 10,000 Bitcoins were exchanged for two pizzas. This event marked the beginning of Bitcoin's journey as a currency.

The Problem Bitcoin Solves

Before Bitcoin, attempts to create digital money had always failed because of the **double-spending problem** - a risk that digital money could be copied and spent multiple times, like duplicating a file on a computer.

How Bitcoin Solved It:

- Bitcoin introduced blockchain, which records all transactions on a transparent, immutable ledger.
- The network uses **consensus mechanisms** to ensure that no one can alter the transaction history or double-spend.

The Idea of Digital Scarcity

In the physical world, scarcity creates value. For example:

- Gold is valuable because it is rare and hard to mine.
- Art by famous painters is valuable because only a limited number of pieces exist.

Satoshi Nakamoto applied the same concept to Bitcoin, creating **digital scarcity**:

- **Fixed Supply:** Only 21 million Bitcoins will ever exist, making it impossible to create more.

- **Mining Process:** Bitcoins are released gradually through mining, which mimics the effort of extracting gold from the ground.

Why Digital Scarcity Matters:

- Unlike fiat money (like dollars), which can be printed in unlimited amounts by governments, Bitcoin's limited supply prevents inflation.

Example: The U.S. Federal Reserve printed trillions of dollars during the 2008 crisis, reducing the value of existing money. Bitcoin eliminates this risk.

- It ensures that Bitcoin remains valuable over time, similar to gold.

Bitcoin as "Digital Gold"

Because of its scarcity and resistance to manipulation, Bitcoin is often called **"digital gold."**

Similarities Between Bitcoin and Gold:

- **Limited Supply:** Only 21 million Bitcoins, just as there is a finite amount of gold on Earth.
- **Mining Process:** Bitcoin mining involves solving complex mathematical problems, similar to the effort required to mine gold.
- **Store of Value:** People use both gold and Bitcoin to protect their wealth from inflation and economic uncertainty.

Differences Between Bitcoin and Gold:

....

32

- **Digital vs. Physical:** Bitcoin exists only on the internet, while gold is tangible.
- **Portability:** Bitcoin is easy to transfer globally in seconds, unlike gold, which is heavy and difficult to move.
- **Divisibility:** Bitcoin can be divided into tiny units (called Satoshis), making it more flexible for small transactions.

Bitcoin's Impact on the Idea of Money

Bitcoin challenged the traditional idea of money by introducing these concepts:

- **Money Without Borders:** Bitcoin is global. It can be sent anywhere in the world without banks or currency exchange fees.

Example: A migrant worker can send money home to their family in minutes, avoiding high fees from companies like Western Union.

- **Trustless Transactions:** Bitcoin doesn't require you to trust a bank or government. Instead, it relies on blockchain technology.

Example: During financial crises, governments can freeze bank accounts. With Bitcoin, only you control your funds.

The Broader Legacy of Bitcoin

Bitcoin wasn't just a new kind of money - it sparked an entire revolution:

- **The Creation of Cryptocurrencies:** Bitcoin inspired thousands of other cryptocurrencies, such as Ethereum and Solana, each with unique features and use cases.
- **Blockchain Innovation:** Bitcoin's blockchain technology has been applied to industries like finance, healthcare and supply chains.
- **The Web3 Movement:** Bitcoin laid the foundation for a decentralized internet, where individuals control their data and assets.

Bitcoin's origins and the concept of digital scarcity have forever changed how we think about money and value. In the next section, we'll explore how other cryptocurrencies expand on Bitcoin's ideas, creating a diverse ecosystem of digital assets for the Web3 world.

Evolution into Smart Contracts and Programmable Money

Bitcoin introduced the idea of a decentralized digital currency, but cryptocurrency has evolved far beyond simple money transfers. The rise of **smart contracts** and **programmable money** has unlocked a world of possibilities, transforming how we interact with money and systems.

From Simple Transactions to Smart Contracts

Bitcoin's blockchain is powerful for securely transferring value. However, it was designed primarily for one purpose: digital cash. Early blockchain developers realized that blockchain technology could do more than store transaction records - it could also automate and execute agreements.

What Are Smart Contracts?

- A **smart contract** is a self-executing program stored on a blockchain. It automatically enforces rules and processes transactions when certain conditions are met.
- Think of it as a digital "if-then" statement: **If condition A is true, then action B will happen.**

Example of a Smart Contract:

- Imagine renting an apartment.
    - You pay the deposit in cryptocurrency.
    - The smart contract verifies the payment and automatically sends you a digital key to access the apartment.

- If you don't pay on time, the contract cancels the key.
- No need for intermediaries like landlords or banks.

The Role of Ethereum in the Evolution

In 2015, Ethereum introduced a blockchain specifically designed to support smart contracts. While Bitcoin is like a calculator - great for solving one specific problem - Ethereum is more like a computer, capable of running any program.

Key Features of Ethereum:

- **Turing Completeness:** Ethereum's programming language, Solidity, allows developers to create complex smart contracts.
- **Decentralized Applications (dApps):** These are software applications that run on the Ethereum blockchain, powered by smart contracts.

Example: Uniswap is a dApp for decentralized trading of cryptocurrencies.

Programmable Money: Beyond Payments

With the introduction of smart contracts, money is no longer just something you send and receive - it can now be **programmed** to perform specific functions.

What Is Programmable Money?
Programmable money refers to cryptocurrency that can carry out predefined actions automatically, based on smart contracts.

....

Examples of Programmable Money in Action:

- **Escrow Services:** Funds are locked in a smart contract and released only when specific conditions are met.

Example: A freelance writer gets paid only after submitting the agreed-upon work.

- **Subscription Services:** A smart contract can automatically deduct payments monthly for services like streaming or storage.
- **Crowdfunding:** Platforms like Kickstarter are being replaced by blockchain-based crowdfunding. Smart contracts return funds to backers if a project doesn't meet its goal.

Real-World Applications of Smart Contracts and Programmable Money

The potential of programmable money goes far beyond simple transactions.

a) Decentralized Finance (DeFi):

- DeFi platforms use smart contracts to provide financial services like lending, borrowing and trading without banks.

Example: On platforms like Aave, users can lend their cryptocurrency and earn interest or borrow against their crypto holdings without needing a credit check.

b) NFTs and Digital Ownership:

- Smart contracts power **non-fungible tokens (NFTs)**, which represent unique digital assets like art, music and collectibles.

Example: An artist can sell their digital artwork as an NFT and automatically receive royalties each time it is resold.

c) Supply Chain Management:

- Smart contracts track goods from production to delivery, ensuring transparency and preventing fraud.

Example: A coffee company can verify the origin of beans and ensure farmers receive fair payment.

d) Insurance:

- Smart contracts can automate insurance claims. If a specific condition is met, the payout happens instantly.

Example: Travel insurance could automatically refund you if your flight is canceled.

Benefits of Smart Contracts and Programmable Money

- **Eliminates Middlemen:** Smart contracts replace brokers, lawyers and banks, reducing costs and increasing efficiency.
- **Faster Transactions:** Automated processes complete tasks in seconds rather than days.
- **Transparency:** Everyone involved can see the terms and conditions on the blockchain.

- **Global Accessibility:** Anyone with internet access can participate, removing barriers like location or financial status.

Challenges and Limitations

While the concept is transformative, it's not without challenges:

- **Complexity:** Writing smart contracts requires technical skills. A poorly coded contract can lead to errors or exploitation.

Example: In 2016, a bug in a smart contract led to the infamous DAO hack, resulting in millions of stolen Ethereum.

- **Scalability:** Current blockchain networks, including Ethereum, can struggle to handle large numbers of transactions quickly.
- **Regulation:** Governments are still figuring out how to regulate programmable money and smart contracts.

The Future of Programmable Money

Smart contracts and programmable money are still in their early stages, but they are evolving rapidly. Emerging innovations include:

- **Layer 2 Solutions:** Technologies like Optimism and Arbitrum reduce congestion on Ethereum, making smart contracts faster and cheaper.
- **Cross-Chain Interoperability:** Future systems will allow smart contracts to interact across different blockchains seamlessly.

- **Real-World Adoption:** As more businesses and governments explore blockchain, programmable money will become a core part of everyday life.

The evolution of cryptocurrency into smart contracts and programmable money marks a significant leap forward. It transforms money from a static tool into a dynamic system that can adapt to countless real-world needs. In the next section, we'll explore how this evolution has created a thriving ecosystem of decentralized applications (dApps) and decentralized finance (DeFi).

Tokenomics: The New Economics of Digital Assets

Types of Tokens: Utility, Governance, Social Tokens, NFTs

The rise of blockchain has given birth to a new type of economy - one built on digital tokens. Tokens are digital assets created and managed on a blockchain. Unlike traditional currencies, tokens have diverse purposes and can represent anything from access rights to ownership.

Let's explore the four major types of tokens: **utility tokens, governance tokens, social tokens** and **non-fungible tokens (NFTs)**.

Utility Tokens: Tools for Access and Use

What Are They?
Utility tokens provide access to a product or service within a blockchain-based ecosystem. Think of them as the "keys" to unlock specific features or functionalities.

Key Features:

- **Access Rights:** Utility tokens often act like membership cards.
- **Limited to a Specific Platform:** They are typically usable only within the ecosystem where they are created.

Examples:

- **Ethereum (ETH):** Used to pay transaction fees on the Ethereum network.
- **Filecoin (FIL):** Lets users buy decentralized storage space on the Filecoin network.
- **Basic Attention Token (BAT):** Rewards users of the Brave browser for viewing ads and can be used to tip creators.

Real-Life Analogy:
Imagine buying a ticket to a concert. The ticket has value because it grants you access to the event, just like utility tokens grant access to blockchain-based services.

Governance Tokens: Power to the People

What Are They?
Governance tokens give holders the right to participate in decision-making within a blockchain project. Token holders can vote on proposals related to upgrades, policies or resource allocation.

Key Features:

- **Decentralized Decision-Making:** Governance tokens shift control from a central authority to the community.
- **Voting Power:** Often, the more tokens you own, the greater your influence in voting.

Examples:

- **Uniswap (UNI):** Lets users vote on changes to the Uniswap protocol, such as fee structures.
- **MakerDAO (MKR):** Token holders decide how the Maker protocol manages its stablecoin, DAI.

Real-Life Analogy:
Owning governance tokens is like being a shareholder in a company. Your tokens give you a voice in the project's future.

Social Tokens: Community and Creator Currency

What Are They?
Social tokens are issued by individuals, communities or creators as a way to build loyalty and reward their supporters. These tokens are often tied to a specific group or influencer and can represent access, rewards or shared ownership.

Key Features:

- **Community-Driven:** They strengthen connections between creators and their audiences.
- **Customizable Utility:** Social tokens can grant access to exclusive content, events or benefits.

Examples:

- **$RAC:** Issued by the musician RAC, this token provides fans with access to exclusive music and events.
- **$FWB (Friends with Benefits):** A token representing membership in a Web3-focused creative community.

Real-Life Analogy:
Social tokens are like loyalty points or fan club memberships, but with real value that can be traded or sold.

Non-Fungible Tokens (NFTs): Unique Digital Ownership

What Are They?

NFTs (non-fungible tokens) are unique digital assets that represent ownership of a specific item or piece of content, such as art, music, videos or virtual real estate. Unlike other tokens, NFTs cannot be exchanged on a one-to-one basis because each token is unique.

Key Features:

- **Uniqueness:** Every NFT has a unique identifier and cannot be replicated.
- **Ownership:** NFTs prove who owns a digital asset, even if the content can be copied.
- **Interoperability:** NFTs can be used across multiple platforms, such as in games or virtual worlds.

Examples:

- **Art and Collectibles:** Beeple's NFT artwork *"Everydays: The First 5000 Days"* sold for $69 million.
- **Gaming:** Axie Infinity NFTs represent characters and assets in the game.
- **Virtual Real Estate:** Platforms like Decentraland let users buy, sell and develop virtual land as NFTs.

Real-Life Analogy:

An NFT is like owning a rare baseball card or a piece of signed art - it has value because of its uniqueness and verifiable authenticity.

Comparing the Four Types of Tokens

Token Type	Purpose	Example
Utility Token	Access to a service or feature	Ethereum (ETH), Filecoin (FIL)
Governance Token	Voting on project decisions	Uniswap (UNI), MakerDAO (MKR)
Social Token	Community engagement and rewards	$RAC, $FWB
NFT	Ownership of unique digital assets	Beeple artwork, Axie Infinity

Why Understanding Tokens Matters

Tokens are more than digital assets; they are the building blocks of the Web3 economy. They enable new forms of participation, ownership and collaboration.

- **Utility Tokens:** Enhance the functionality of blockchain platforms.
- **Governance Tokens:** Give people a say in decentralized systems.
- **Social Tokens:** Empower creators and communities.
- **NFTs:** Redefine ownership in the digital age.

As the Web3 ecosystem grows, tokens will play an even greater role in shaping how we interact with technology, finance and culture.

In the next section, we'll explore how tokenomics influences the design of these tokens, ensuring sustainability and value creation in the digital economy.

Basics of Token Design and Value Creation

Tokenomics or the economics of tokens, is central to understanding how digital assets work and gain value. Successful token design combines technology, economics and game theory to ensure that a token serves its purpose while maintaining long-term value for its holders.

What Is Token Design?

Token design refers to the process of defining the structure, purpose and mechanics of a token within a blockchain ecosystem. A well-designed token aligns the interests of users, investors and the broader community.

Key Aspects of Token Design:

- **Purpose:** What role does the token serve?
- **Supply:** How many tokens will exist?
- **Distribution:** How are tokens allocated to participants?
- **Incentives:** How does the token encourage desired behaviors?

Example:
In a decentralized finance (DeFi) project, tokens might incentivize users to provide liquidity or stake their holdings.

Token Supply: Scarcity and Inflation

The supply of a token is a critical factor in its design. A token's value often depends on its scarcity and how supply changes over time.

Types of Supply Models:

1. **Fixed Supply:** The total number of tokens is capped, creating scarcity.

Example: Bitcoin (BTC) has a maximum supply of 21 million coins.

Effect: Encourages long-term holding as the asset becomes scarcer.

2. **Inflationary Supply:** New tokens are continuously created, often as rewards for network participants.

Example: Ethereum (ETH) has no fixed supply but controls inflation through token burns and upgrades.

Effect: Balances demand by rewarding active users but requires careful management to avoid devaluation.

3. **Deflationary Supply:** Tokens are intentionally removed from circulation over time.

Example: Binance Coin (BNB) regularly burns tokens to reduce supply and increase value.

Token Distribution: Fairness and Participation

How tokens are distributed impacts both the project's success and the trust of its community.

Methods of Distribution:

- **Pre-Mined Tokens:** Tokens are created before the project launches and distributed to founders, investors and early supporters.
    - **Pros:** Provides initial funding for development.
    - **Cons:** Can lead to centralization if a few entities control most of the supply.
- **Mining or Staking Rewards:** Tokens are earned by participants who contribute resources or secure the network.

Example: Bitcoin miners earn tokens by validating transactions.

- **Airdrops:** Free tokens are distributed to users to encourage adoption or reward early participation.

Example: Uniswap (UNI) airdropped tokens to its early users, creating a loyal community.

- **Token Sales (ICO, IEO, IDO):** Tokens are sold to raise funds for the project.

Example: Ethereum raised $18 million through an initial coin offering (ICO) in 2014.

Mechanisms for Value Creation

Tokens derive value from utility, demand and scarcity. Effective mechanisms ensure that the token's use case drives adoption and builds value over time.

a) Utility:
The more useful a token is, the greater its demand.

Example: Binance Coin (BNB) reduces trading fees on the Binance exchange, making it valuable to frequent traders.

b) Network Effect:
As more people join a network, the value of its token increases.

Example: Ethereum's token, ETH, benefits from the growing number of decentralized applications (dApps) built on its network.

c) Governance and Voting Power:
Tokens that grant voting rights can gain value as the network grows.

Example: MakerDAO's MKR token allows holders to shape the future of the protocol, increasing its appeal.

d) Rewards and Incentives:
Many tokens reward holders or users for participating in the ecosystem.

Example: DeFi projects like Compound distribute tokens to users who provide liquidity or borrow funds, creating demand for their token.

e) Burn Mechanisms:
Burning tokens (removing them permanently) creates scarcity and increases value.

Example: Shiba Inu (SHIB) periodically burns tokens to reduce its massive supply and stabilize its price.

Token Governance and Sustainability

Tokens should be designed to ensure long-term sustainability. Poor tokenomics can lead to a collapse in value or loss of community trust.

Challenges in Token Design:

- **Over-Distribution:** If too many tokens are distributed too quickly, their value may plummet.
- **Lack of Use Case:** Tokens without clear utility risk becoming speculative assets with no real value.
- **Centralization:** If too many tokens are held by a small group, the project can lose its decentralized appeal.

Solutions for Sustainable Tokenomics:

- **Vesting Periods:** Releasing tokens to team members and early investors over time prevents sudden sell-offs.
- **Dynamic Rewards:** Adjusting staking or mining rewards based on network activity helps maintain engagement.
- **Transparent Governance:** Decentralized decision-making builds trust and encourages participation.

Real-World Example: Ethereum's Transition to Proof-of-Stake

Ethereum's recent transition to **Proof-of-Stake (PoS)** demonstrates how tokenomics can evolve to meet a network's needs.

- **Old Model (Proof-of-Work):** Miners earned ETH by validating transactions, which consumed large amounts of energy.
- **New Model (Proof-of-Stake):** Users stake ETH to secure the network and earn rewards, reducing energy consumption and aligning incentives.

This shift made Ethereum's tokenomics more sustainable and environmentally friendly while ensuring the network's security.

The Role of Tokenomics in the Web3 Economy

In the Web3 ecosystem, tokens are not just financial instruments - they are tools for participation, governance and innovation.

- **For Developers:** Tokenomics funds projects and incentivizes early adopters.
- **For Users:** Tokens offer tangible rewards for participation and loyalty.
- **For Communities:** They enable decentralized ownership and decision-making.

Understanding the basics of token design and value creation is crucial for anyone navigating the Web3 economy. A well-designed token can empower communities, sustain projects and redefine how we think about value in the digital age.

In the next section, we'll delve deeper into how tokenomics intersects with decentralized finance (DeFi) and its transformative potential.

Part II: Printing Your Own Currency

What Does "Printing Your Currency" Mean in Web3?

From Central Banks to Personal Tokenization

In the traditional financial system, the ability to "print money" is tightly controlled by central banks. These institutions create and manage national currencies, deciding how much money enters the economy. However, Web3 disrupts this paradigm. In the world of blockchain and decentralized technologies, individuals and communities can create their own forms of currency - tokens - that serve specific purposes and hold value within their ecosystems.

Let's explore the journey from central bank-issued currencies to the personal tokenization made possible by Web3.

The Role of Central Banks in Traditional Currency Printing

Central banks, like the Federal Reserve in the U.S. or the European Central Bank, control the supply of money in an economy.

- **How Do They Print Money?**
  Central banks can create money digitally or physically. They use tools like interest rate adjustments and quantitative easing to inject liquidity into the economy.
- **Why Do They Have This Power?**
  Governments rely on central banks to maintain economic stability, control inflation and support growth. However, this power comes with risks:
    - **Overprinting:** Excessive money supply can lead to inflation, reducing the purchasing power of citizens.

- Lack of Transparency: Decisions are often made by a small group of policymakers, leaving the public with limited insight.

Example: During the COVID-19 pandemic, central banks worldwide printed trillions of dollars to stimulate their economies, leading to debates about long-term economic impacts.

How Web3 Changes the Paradigm

Web3 flips the traditional model by decentralizing the power to create currency. In this new framework, anyone can "print" their own currency by creating a token on a blockchain.

What Is Personal Tokenization?

Personal tokenization refers to the creation of digital tokens that represent value, utility or ownership tied to an individual, community or specific purpose.

- **No Central Authority:** Instead of relying on central banks, token issuance is governed by smart contracts and blockchain protocols.
- **Global Access:** Anyone with internet access can create, distribute and trade tokens.
- **Tailored Economics:** Tokens can be designed with specific rules, such as fixed supply or rewards for certain behaviors.

Types of Personal and Community Tokens

a) Personal Tokens:
Individuals can issue tokens to represent their personal brand, skills or future value.

Example: An artist might create a token that grants holders access to exclusive artwork or events.

b) Community Tokens:
Communities and organizations can issue tokens to incentivize participation and build loyalty.

Example: A fitness club could create tokens that members earn for attending workouts, which can then be exchanged for merchandise.

c) Functional Tokens:
Tokens designed for specific purposes, such as paying for services, voting on decisions or accessing digital assets.

Examples of Personal Tokenization in Action

a) Creators and Influencers:
Artists, musicians and influencers can tokenize their work and offer fans a stake in their success.

Example: Musician RAC launched the $RAC token, allowing fans to access exclusive content and experiences.

b) Community Empowerment:
Grassroots organizations can create tokens to fund projects and reward participation.

Example: CityDAO, a decentralized community, issues tokens to represent ownership of physical land parcels.

c) Startups and Entrepreneurs:
Instead of seeking traditional funding, startups can issue tokens to raise capital and reward early supporters.

Example: Ethereum itself was funded through an initial coin offering (ICO), where participants purchased ETH tokens before the network launched.

Benefits of Personal Tokenization

- **Financial Sovereignty:** Individuals gain control over their own economic value, bypassing traditional financial intermediaries.
- **Global Reach:** Tokens can be traded and used anywhere in the world, creating new opportunities for cross-border collaboration.
- **Direct Relationships:** Creators and communities can connect directly with supporters without relying on platforms or agencies.

Challenges and Risks

While personal tokenization is empowering, it comes with challenges:

- **Over-Supply Risk:** Printing too many tokens without clear utility can dilute their value.
- **Regulatory Uncertainty:** Governments may regulate personal and community tokens as securities, adding legal complexities.
- **Trust Issues:** If token creators don't deliver on promises, trust can erode, harming both reputation and token value.

The Future of Personal Tokenization

As Web3 technologies mature, personal tokenization could redefine the way we think about value, work and ownership.

- **For Individuals:** Tokenization can transform how people monetize their skills, time and creativity.
- **For Communities:** Local economies can flourish with bespoke tokens tailored to their specific needs.
- **For the World:** By decentralizing currency creation, Web3 fosters a more inclusive and equitable financial system.

In the next chapter, we'll dive into **how you can create and design your own currency**, exploring the technical and practical steps involved in bringing your token to life.

Examples: Creators, Communities and DAOs Launching Tokens

One of the most exciting aspects of Web3 is the ability for creators, communities and decentralized autonomous organizations (DAOs) to issue their own tokens. These tokens empower individuals and groups to establish economic systems, reward participation and create new value streams. Let's explore how these entities are already leveraging tokenization to reshape their industries and communities.

Creators: Monetizing Talent and Building Direct Relationships

Creators such as artists, musicians, writers and influencers are using tokens to connect with their audiences in innovative ways.

- **How It Works:**
  A creator issues a token that represents access, rewards or shared ownership of their work or brand. Supporters buy or earn these tokens to engage with exclusive content, events or benefits.

Examples:

- **RAC ($RAC):**
  The Grammy-winning musician RAC launched a social token to reward his fans. Holders of $RAC can access exclusive music, merchandise and experiences, creating a closer connection between RAC and his supporters.
- **WhaleShark ($WHALE):**
  A digital art collector issued $WHALE tokens backed

by a vault of rare NFTs. Token holders gain access to the art collection and community events.
- **Paris Hilton's NFTs:**
Paris Hilton released NFTs representing her digital art. These NFTs provide collectors with unique ownership of her work while showcasing the potential of Web3 for creators.

Communities: Empowering Grassroots Economies

Communities are launching tokens to incentivize participation, foster loyalty and create shared ownership.

- **How It Works:**
Community tokens often reward members for contributing value, such as engaging in discussions, completing tasks or promoting the group. These tokens can be used within the community or traded externally.

Examples:

- **Friends with Benefits ($FWB):**
This exclusive Web3 social club issues $FWB tokens to grant membership. Members use tokens to access events, discussions and collaborations. The token's value grows as the community thrives.
- **Bankless DAO ($BANK):**
A community focused on educating people about Web3 issues $BANK tokens. Members earn tokens by contributing content, hosting workshops or participating in governance.
- **Local Economies with Tokens:**
Communities like Circular Economy in Kenya use

tokens to encourage trading goods and services locally, fostering economic resilience.

DAOs: Decentralized Governance and Shared Ownership

Decentralized Autonomous Organizations (DAOs) use tokens to represent governance rights, ownership stakes and incentives for participation.

- **How It Works:**
  DAOs issue tokens that allow holders to vote on proposals, allocate funds and shape the project's future. These tokens align participants' incentives and distribute power democratically.

Examples:

- **Uniswap ($UNI):**
  Uniswap, a decentralized exchange, issued $UNI tokens to its users. Holders can vote on key decisions, such as protocol upgrades or fee structures, giving them a say in the platform's governance.
- **CityDAO:**
  CityDAO is creating a decentralized approach to owning and managing land. Its token holders collectively decide how to use and develop land parcels in Wyoming, USA.
- **MakerDAO ($MKR):**
  MakerDAO's MKR token allows holders to govern the protocol that manages the DAI stablecoin. Decisions include risk parameters, collateral types and system upgrades.

Benefits of Tokenization for Creators, Communities and DAOs

- **Direct Relationships:** Tokens remove intermediaries, enabling direct interaction between creators/communities and their supporters.
- **Incentive Alignment:** Tokens reward participants who contribute to the ecosystem's growth and success.
- **Ownership and Governance:** Token holders gain a stake in the ecosystem, fostering loyalty and active involvement.
- **Global Reach:** Blockchain technology ensures tokens can be accessed and traded worldwide.

Challenges and Considerations

While tokenization offers immense potential, it comes with challenges:

- **Regulation:** Creators and communities must navigate legal requirements, as some tokens may be classified as securities.
- **Value Stability:** The value of tokens can be volatile, potentially affecting trust and adoption.
- **Sustainability:** Poorly designed tokens can fail to maintain long-term utility or value.

The Future of Tokenized Economies

As Web3 adoption grows, more creators, communities and DAOs will embrace tokenization to unlock new opportunities. Tokens will become essential tools for building digital-first economies that are decentralized, transparent and participatory.

In the next section, we'll explore how **you can create your own token** and design a sustainable economy around it, unlocking the power of personal tokenization in Web3.

Designing a Personal or Community Token

Purpose: Why Launch a Token?

Creating a token isn't just about joining the blockchain movement; it's about solving real problems, building communities and empowering individuals. Before designing a token, it's crucial to define its purpose clearly. A well-defined purpose ensures that the token serves a meaningful role in its ecosystem, attracting users and sustaining its value over time.

Identifying the Core Purpose

The purpose of your token should address a specific need or opportunity. Here are some common motivations for launching a token:

a) Incentivizing Participation:
Tokens can reward users for contributing to a project or community.

Example: In a fitness app, users might earn tokens for completing workouts or hitting health goals.

b) Building Loyalty:
Tokens can create a sense of belonging and encourage long-term engagement.

Example: A gaming platform could issue tokens that players use to unlock exclusive levels or skins.

c) Enabling Governance:
Tokens can give holders the right to vote on decisions within a decentralized organization or project.

Example: A DAO might issue tokens that let members decide on funding proposals or partnerships.

d) Fundraising:
Tokens can help raise funds for a project or cause while giving supporters a stake in its success.

Example: A startup might sell tokens to fund development, offering early backers benefits or profits in return.

e) Representing Ownership:
Tokens can represent ownership of physical or digital assets.

Example: A token might represent a share in a co-working space, giving holders access and a say in its management.

f) Creating a Digital Economy:
Tokens can act as currency within a specific ecosystem.

Example: A social media platform might issue tokens to reward creators and allow users to purchase premium content.

Personal Tokens: A Gateway to Empowerment

Personal tokens focus on an individual's skills, work or reputation. Their purpose might include:

- Raising funds for personal projects.
- Rewarding supporters with exclusive perks or content.
- Creating a direct economic connection between the creator and their audience.

Example:

- **Alex Masmej's $ALEX Token:**
  Alex, a young entrepreneur, launched a personal token to fund his move to Silicon Valley. Token holders received a share of his future earnings and access to his journey.

Community Tokens: Strengthening Bonds and Shared Ownership

For communities, tokens serve as tools for engagement, collaboration and shared ownership. They are designed to:

- **Unite Members:** Tokens give members a shared identity and purpose.
- **Reward Contributions:** Active participation earns tokens, motivating members to contribute.
- **Fund Initiatives:** Tokens can be sold to fund community projects and events.

Example:

- **Friends with Benefits ($FWB):** This social community uses its token to grant membership, aligning its growth with the interests of its token holders.

Aligning Purpose with Ecosystem Design

Once the token's purpose is clear, it should align with the broader goals of the ecosystem. Consider these factors:

- **Utility:** How will the token be used in day-to-day interactions?

- **Sustainability:** Can the token maintain its value and utility over time?
- **Scalability:** Can the token support growth in users and transactions?

Purpose Drives Tokenomics

A token's purpose directly influences its design and economics:

- **Fixed Supply for Scarcity:** Tokens designed for fundraising or digital scarcity may have a capped supply, driving demand.
- **Inflationary Supply for Incentives:** Tokens meant to reward participation might use controlled inflation to sustain rewards.
- **Burn Mechanisms for Stability:** Some tokens implement burning mechanisms to reduce supply and stabilize value.

Example:

- **Binance Coin (BNB):** Initially designed to reduce trading fees on Binance, BNB has expanded its utility to include governance, rewards and transaction fees, aligning with Binance's growing ecosystem.

Testing the Purpose with Questions

Before launching your token, ask:

- What problem does this token solve?
- Who will benefit from using the token?

- How does the token align with the goals of the project or community?
- Will the token retain its value and utility as the ecosystem evolves?

Clear answers to these questions will help ensure that your token is not only functional but also valuable to its intended audience.

In the next section, we'll discuss **the technical and strategic aspects of token creation**, including choosing the right blockchain, designing supply models and ensuring long-term success.

Key Considerations: Supply, Utility and Governance

Designing a successful token requires thoughtful planning. A poorly designed token can lose value, fail to gain adoption or harm trust in the ecosystem. By carefully considering key elements like supply, utility and governance, you can create a token that serves its purpose effectively and sustainably.

Supply: Managing Scarcity and Abundance

Supply refers to the number of tokens created and how they're distributed over time.
Determining the right supply model is critical, as it affects demand, value and user behavior.

a) Fixed Supply:

- **What It Is:** A predetermined number of tokens are created and no more can be issued.
- **Benefits:** Creates scarcity, driving demand and increasing value over time.

Example: Bitcoin has a fixed supply of 21 million coins, which contributes to its status as a store of value.

b) Inflationary Supply:

- **What It Is:** New tokens are continuously minted, often at a controlled rate.
- **Benefits:** Supports ongoing incentives and rewards for ecosystem participants.

Example: Ethereum's network issues new ETH through staking rewards to incentivize validators.

c) **Deflationary Mechanisms:**

- **What It Is:** Tokens are removed from circulation over time, reducing supply. This can happen through mechanisms like token burning.
- **Benefits:** Helps maintain or increase token value by limiting availability.

Example: Binance Coin (BNB) uses token burns to reduce supply, increasing scarcity.

Questions to Ask:

- How many tokens should exist initially?
- Should additional tokens be issued in the future?
- If inflation is allowed, how will it be managed to prevent devaluation?

Utility: Defining How the Token Is Used

Utility refers to the token's role and purpose within its ecosystem. A token with clear and valuable utility attracts users and ensures its relevance over time.

a) Payment Token:
Tokens can act as currency for transactions within a specific ecosystem.

Example: $SAND is used in The Sandbox to buy virtual land and assets.

b) Access Token:
Tokens can grant access to services, events or exclusive content.

Example: $FWB tokens give holders access to the Friends with Benefits social community.

c) Governance Token:
Tokens can enable holders to participate in decision-making processes.

Example: Uniswap's $UNI token allows holders to vote on protocol upgrades and resource allocation.

d) Reward Token:
Tokens can incentivize desired actions, such as contributing to a project or using a platform.

Example: Steemit rewards users with tokens for creating and curating content.

e) Asset-Backed Token:
Tokens can represent ownership of a physical or digital asset.

Example: Tether (USDT) is a stablecoin backed by fiat reserves.

Questions to Ask:

- What primary function will the token serve?
- Will it have multiple utilities?
- How will the utility evolve as the ecosystem grows?

Governance: Ensuring Fair Decision-Making

Governance refers to how decisions about the token and ecosystem are made. Clear governance mechanisms ensure transparency, fairness and adaptability over time.

a) Centralized Governance:
Decisions are made by a small group, such as the token creator or core team.

- **Benefits:** Faster decision-making and tighter control.
- **Challenges:** May lack transparency or alienate users seeking decentralization.

b) Decentralized Governance:
Token holders collectively decide on proposals, often using smart contracts for voting.

- **Benefits:** Promotes transparency and aligns with Web3 principles of shared ownership.
- **Challenges:** Requires active participation from the community to function effectively.

c) Hybrid Governance:
Combines centralized and decentralized approaches, with a

core team managing early decisions before transitioning to community governance.

- **Benefits:** Balances efficiency with community involvement.

Examples:

- **MakerDAO:** Holders of $MKR vote on changes to the protocol, such as adding new collateral types for its DAI stablecoin.
- **Compound:** Holders of $COMP propose and vote on updates to the lending protocol.

Questions to Ask:

- Who will have the authority to make key decisions initially?
- Should governance transition to the community over time?
- How will token holders participate in governance (e.g., voting systems)?

Bringing It All Together

A well-designed token balances supply, utility and governance:

- **Supply:** Determines scarcity and long-term economic viability.
- **Utility:** Defines the token's purpose and attracts users to the ecosystem.
- **Governance:** Ensures fairness, transparency and adaptability as the project grows.

By addressing these considerations thoughtfully, you can create a token that serves its purpose effectively while fostering trust and engagement.

In the next section, we'll explore **practical steps to launch a token**, from choosing the right blockchain to creating smart contracts and distributing your currency.

Tools and Platforms

Overview of Tools Like Ethereum, Solana, Binance Smart Chain and Layer 2 Solutions

Creating and launching a token requires choosing the right blockchain and tools. Each blockchain platform offers unique features, capabilities and trade-offs that can significantly influence the success of your project. Here, we explore some of the most popular platforms and their role in token creation.

Ethereum: The Pioneer of Smart Contracts

Overview:
Ethereum is the first blockchain to introduce smart contracts, enabling programmable money and decentralized applications (dApps). It remains the most widely used platform for token creation and decentralized finance (DeFi).

Features:

- **ERC Standards:** Ethereum offers standard token frameworks like ERC-20 (fungible tokens) and ERC-721/ERC-1155 (NFTs).
- **Robust Ecosystem:** Thousands of projects and tools, such as MetaMask and Remix, support Ethereum-based development.
- **Decentralization:** One of the most decentralized and secure blockchains.

Challenges:

- **High Gas Fees:** Transactions can be expensive during network congestion.

- **Scalability Issues:** Limited throughput, although Ethereum 2.0 and Layer 2 solutions are addressing this.

Best For:

- Complex tokenized ecosystems with high security needs.
- Projects requiring robust DeFi integrations.

Solana: High-Speed and Low-Cost Transactions

Overview:
Solana is a blockchain known for its high throughput and low transaction costs, making it an attractive option for scalable applications.

Features:

- **High Performance:** Processes up to 65,000 transactions per second (TPS).
- **Low Fees:** Average transaction cost is a fraction of a cent.
- **Developer-Friendly:** Tools like Solana Program Library (SPL) simplify token creation.

Challenges:

- **Decentralization Concerns:** Relatively low number of validators compared to Ethereum.
- **Downtime Issues:** The network has experienced outages, raising reliability concerns.

Best For:

- Projects requiring frequent microtransactions, like gaming or social tokens.
- NFT platforms with high transaction volumes.

Binance Smart Chain (BSC): Affordable and Ethereum-Compatible

Overview:
BSC is a blockchain launched by Binance, designed for fast and low-cost transactions. It is compatible with Ethereum's development tools, making it easy to migrate projects.

Features:

- **Low Costs:** Transactions are inexpensive, ideal for users on a budget.
- **Ethereum Compatibility:** Supports the same smart contract standards as Ethereum (e.g., BEP-20 mirrors ERC-20).
- **Vibrant Ecosystem:** Hosts a variety of DeFi platforms, NFT marketplaces and tokens.

Challenges:

- **Centralization:** BSC is operated by a relatively small number of validators, raising concerns about governance and security.
- **Scalability Limits:** Although faster than Ethereum, BSC's performance may still struggle under heavy loads.

Best For:

- Budget-conscious creators looking for Ethereum-like functionality.

- DeFi projects that need fast and affordable transactions.

Layer 2 Solutions: Scaling Ethereum

Overview:

Layer 2 solutions are built on top of Ethereum to improve scalability and reduce costs without compromising decentralization.

Examples:

- **Polygon (MATIC):** A popular Layer 2 solution offering fast and affordable transactions with strong developer tools.
- **Arbitrum:** Focused on rollups to scale Ethereum, enabling seamless integration with Ethereum dApps.
- **Optimism:** Another rollup-based solution optimized for Ethereum scaling.

Features:

- **Cost-Effective:** Significantly lower gas fees compared to the Ethereum mainnet.
- **Seamless Interoperability:** Easy to transfer tokens between Ethereum and Layer 2 networks.
- **Decentralization Retained:** Operates under Ethereum's security framework.

Challenges:

- **Ecosystem Maturity:** Fewer dApps and users compared to Ethereum mainnet.
- **Learning Curve:** Developers may need to adapt their tools and processes.

Best For:

- Projects aiming for Ethereum's security with reduced transaction costs.

- DeFi or gaming applications requiring high throughput.

Choosing the Right Platform for Your Token

When deciding on a blockchain, consider:

1. **Transaction Costs:**
   - If your token will be used frequently (e.g., gaming or social tokens), prioritize platforms with low fees like Solana or BSC.
2. **Ecosystem Support:**
   - For projects relying on established DeFi tools or integrations, Ethereum and its Layer 2 solutions are ideal.
3. **Decentralization vs. Speed:**
   - If decentralization is critical, Ethereum may be the best choice. For speed and efficiency, Solana or BSC are strong contenders.
4. **Target Audience:**
   - Consider the familiarity and preferences of your user base. Ethereum is well-known, while newer platforms like Solana might appeal to tech-savvy users.

In the next section, we'll guide you through **the step-by-step process of creating and launching your token** on the platform of your choice, ensuring a smooth and successful launch.

No-Code Options for Launching Tokens

You no longer need advanced coding skills to create and launch your own token. Several platforms offer no-code solutions that simplify the process, making token creation accessible to creators, communities and entrepreneurs. These tools allow users to focus on their token's purpose and design without worrying about the complexities of blockchain programming.

Why Choose a No-Code Solution?

No-code platforms are ideal for:

- **Speed:** Quickly launching tokens without needing to write or audit smart contracts.
- **Accessibility:** Democratizing token creation for non-technical individuals.
- **Affordability:** Reducing costs associated with hiring developers.
- **Ease of Use:** Intuitive interfaces guide users through the token creation process.

Popular No-Code Platforms for Token Creation

a) CoinTool

- **Overview:**
  CoinTool provides a simple interface for creating tokens on multiple blockchains, including Ethereum, Binance Smart Chain (BSC) and Polygon.
- **Key Features:**

- o Choose token standards like ERC-20 or BEP-20.
- o Set token name, symbol, supply and decimals.
- o Supports various networks for flexibility.
- **Best For:**
  Beginners who want a quick and straightforward way to create basic tokens.

b) Moralis Money

- **Overview:**
  Moralis Money is part of the Moralis Web3 development suite, offering no-code token creation alongside advanced blockchain tools.
- **Key Features:**
  - o Simple token creation on Ethereum and Binance Smart Chain.
  - o Integration with Moralis's backend for managing dApps.
  - o Customizable tokenomics features.
- **Best For:**
  Creators who may expand into building dApps or ecosystems later.

c) DxLaunch (by DxSale)

- **Overview:**
  A decentralized platform for creating and launching tokens with built-in crowdfunding features.
- **Key Features:**
  - o Create tokens on Ethereum, BSC and other chains.
  - o Integrated presale and launchpad for fundraising.
  - o Liquidity lock options for added trust.

- **Best For:**
  Projects looking to combine token creation with fundraising.

d) Create My Token

- **Overview:**
  A user-friendly platform specifically designed for non-technical users.
- **Key Features:**
  - Token creation on Ethereum and Binance Smart Chain.
  - Simple sliders to adjust supply and other parameters.
  - Free and paid options depending on the level of customization.
- **Best For:**
  Individuals or communities starting with minimal upfront investment.

e) Mintable (for NFTs)

- **Overview:**
  Mintable specializes in creating and launching NFTs (non-fungible tokens) without requiring coding skills.
- **Key Features:**
  - Create, mint and sell NFTs on Ethereum or Immutable X.
  - Supports artwork, music and digital collectibles.
  - Royalty options for ongoing revenue.
- **Best For:**
  Creators interested in tokenizing digital assets like art or music.

Key Steps in No-Code Token Creation

Using these platforms typically involves the following steps:

1. **Select a Blockchain:** Choose a blockchain based on your needs (e.g., Ethereum for robust tools, Solana for low fees).
2. **Define Token Parameters:**
    - **Name and Symbol:** Choose a unique name and ticker (e.g., $MYTOKEN).
    - **Total Supply:** Determine the number of tokens to create.
    - **Decimals:** Set the smallest unit of the token (e.g., 18 decimals for Ethereum).
3. **Customize Tokenomics:** Adjust features like minting, burning or distribution mechanisms.
4. **Deploy the Token:** The platform generates the smart contract and deploys it to the blockchain.
5. **Promote and List:** List your token on decentralized exchanges (DEXs) or launchpads.

Advantages and Limitations of No-Code Tools

Advantages:

- **Quick Start:** Launch tokens in minutes.
- **No Programming Required:** Reduces technical barriers.
- **Affordable:** Often free or low-cost compared to custom development.

Limitations:

- **Customization:** Advanced features like governance or complex tokenomics may not be available.

- **Security:** Standardized templates may be less secure than custom-audited smart contracts.
- **Scalability:** May not support high-demand or enterprise-level projects.

Use Cases for No-Code Token Creation

- **Personal Tokens:** Launch a token to represent your brand, time or expertise.
- **Community Tokens:** Unite and reward members of a group or online community.
- **Event Tickets:** Tokenize event access for secure and transparent ticketing.
- **Crowdfunding:** Create tokens for raising funds and rewarding backers.
- **NFT Drops:** Tokenize digital art, music or collectibles for sale or auction.

No-code tools are transforming token creation into an accessible process for everyone. Whether you're a creator launching a personal token, a community leader building shared value or a project founder testing a concept, these platforms provide an excellent starting point.

In the next section, we'll discuss **strategies for distributing and promoting your token**, ensuring that it reaches your intended audience effectively.

Part III: Use Cases and Real-World Examples

Creator Economies: Empowering Artists and Influencers

Case Studies: Social Tokens and NFTs

The rise of Web3 has unlocked unprecedented opportunities for artists, influencers and content creators to monetize their work and build direct relationships with their audiences. Social tokens and non-fungible tokens (NFTs) have emerged as two key innovations driving this transformation. Through these tools, creators can establish their own economies, incentivize community participation and capture more value from their work.

Social Tokens: Redefining Community Engagement

Social tokens are blockchain-based digital currencies tied to an individual, group or brand. They enable creators to build an economy around their persona or community, allowing fans and followers to invest in their success.

Case Study 1: $FWB (Friends With Benefits)

- **What It Is:**
  $FWB is a social token for an exclusive online community of artists, creators and crypto enthusiasts. Members need $FWB tokens to access the community.
- **How It Works:**
    - Token holders can participate in events, vote on community decisions and collaborate on projects.

- ○ The token incentivizes active engagement, as its value grows with the community's success.
- **Impact:**
  $FWB showcases how a token can unify like-minded individuals and create a thriving digital culture.

Case Study 2: $RAC (RAC Token)

- **What It Is:**
  $RAC is a social token launched by Grammy-winning artist RAC (André Allen Anjos) to reward fans and supporters.
- **How It Works:**
  - ○ Fans earn $RAC for supporting the artist, sharing content or participating in the community.
  - ○ Token holders receive exclusive benefits, such as early access to music, merchandise and special events.
- **Impact:**
  $RAC empowers fans to participate directly in RAC's career, fostering a sense of ownership and deeper connection.

NFTs: Ownership and Monetization in the Digital Age

Non-fungible tokens (NFTs) are unique digital assets that represent ownership of a specific item, such as art, music, videos or virtual goods. By using blockchain technology, NFTs provide verifiable ownership, scarcity and resale potential for digital creations.

Case Study 1: Beeple's "Everydays: The First 5000 Days"

- **What It Is:**
  A digital artwork by artist Beeple (Mike Winkelmann), sold as an NFT for $69.3 million at a Christie's auction.
- **How It Works:**
  - The NFT certifies ownership of the digital collage, even though the image itself is widely available online.
  - Beeple retained a percentage of resale royalties, ensuring continued earnings as the artwork appreciates.
- **Impact:**
  This sale validated NFTs as a legitimate medium for high-value art and introduced blockchain to traditional art markets.

Case Study 2: Kings of Leon's NFT Album

- **What It Is:**
  The band Kings of Leon released their album *When You See Yourself* as an NFT, offering exclusive perks to buyers.
- **How It Works:**
  - Fans could purchase NFTs that included digital downloads, limited-edition vinyl and lifetime concert passes.
  - The NFTs created a direct relationship between the band and their fans, bypassing traditional record labels.
- **Impact:**
  This initiative demonstrated how musicians can use NFTs to monetize their work creatively and reward loyal fans.

Case Study 3: Bored Ape Yacht Club (BAYC)

- **What It Is:**
  A collection of 10,000 unique NFTs featuring cartoon apes, BAYC has become a cultural phenomenon and status symbol.
- **How It Works:**
  - Owners of BAYC NFTs gain access to exclusive benefits, such as private events, merchandise and collaborative projects.
  - The NFTs are resellable and some have fetched millions of dollars on secondary markets.
- **Impact:**
  BAYC demonstrates how NFTs can evolve into social clubs and lifestyle brands, transcending their initial purpose.

Comparing Social Tokens and NFTs

Feature	Social Tokens	NFTs
Purpose	Currency for a creator's community	Ownership of unique digital assets
Utility	Access to benefits, voting or rewards	Proof of ownership, scarcity and royalties
Example	$RAC for exclusive music access	Beeple's NFT artwork
Monetization	Token value grows with creator success	Direct sales and royalties

Challenges and Opportunities

Challenges:

- **Market Volatility:** Token values can fluctuate, affecting the creator's economy.
- **Access Barriers:** Fans may find blockchain tools or wallets confusing.
- **Oversaturation:** The NFT space is crowded, making it harder to stand out.

Opportunities:

- **Direct Monetization:** Creators retain a larger share of their earnings compared to traditional platforms.
- **Fan Engagement:** Tokens and NFTs foster deeper relationships with audiences.
- **New Revenue Streams:** Royalties, memberships and resale markets offer long-term earnings.

Social tokens and NFTs are revolutionizing the creator economy by empowering individuals to take control of their work and monetize it in new ways. These tools not only provide financial independence but also enable creators to build stronger, more engaged communities.

In the next section, we'll explore **community-driven use cases**, including how decentralized autonomous organizations (DAOs) are leveraging blockchain to create shared economies and achieve collective goals.

Community Economies

DAOs and Shared Value Systems

Decentralized Autonomous Organizations (DAOs) are transforming how communities collaborate, govern and create shared value. By leveraging blockchain technology, DAOs empower groups of people to pool resources, make decisions collectively and distribute rewards transparently. This new model of community-driven economies has vast implications for businesses, social movements and online communities.

What Is a DAO?

A **Decentralized Autonomous Organization (DAO)** is a group of people organized around a shared purpose, operating transparently on a blockchain. DAOs use smart contracts to automate processes like voting, funding and governance, removing the need for traditional hierarchies or intermediaries.

- **Key Features:**
    - **Decentralization:** Power is distributed among members, not controlled by a central authority.
    - **Transparency:** All transactions and decisions are recorded on the blockchain.
    - **Automation:** Smart contracts enforce rules and execute agreements without manual oversight.

How DAOs Create Shared Value Systems

DAOs are designed to align incentives among members. Here's how they achieve shared value:

- **Token-Based Governance:** Members hold tokens that represent voting power and ownership in the DAO.
- **Collective Decision-Making:** Proposals are submitted and members vote to determine actions.
- **Profit Sharing:** Revenue generated by the DAO is distributed among members based on their contributions or holdings.

Real-World Examples of DAOs

a) MakerDAO: The Pioneer of DeFi

- **What It Is:**
  MakerDAO is a decentralized finance (DeFi) platform that manages the stablecoin DAI, which is pegged to the US dollar.
- **How It Works:**
    - MakerDAO token holders vote on key decisions, such as interest rates and collateral requirements.
    - The system is governed entirely by its community without centralized control.
- **Impact:**
  MakerDAO has created a stable, decentralized currency and empowered its members to manage a global financial ecosystem.

b) ConstitutionDAO: Crowdfunding for a Common Goal

- **What It Is:**
  ConstitutionDAO was a temporary DAO formed to bid on a rare copy of the U.S. Constitution at auction.
- **How It Works:**
  - Members contributed funds in exchange for governance tokens.
  - Although the group lost the auction, contributors were refunded or allowed to keep tokens as a memento.
- **Impact:**
  This DAO demonstrated the potential of collective action for shared cultural goals.

c) Krause House DAO: Fan-Owned Sports Teams

- **What It Is:**
  Krause House is a DAO aiming to purchase and operate an NBA team collectively.
- **How It Works:**
  - Members pool resources and vote on team-related decisions.
  - Governance tokens give fans a say in how the team is run.
- **Impact:**
  Krause House exemplifies how DAOs can disrupt traditional ownership models in sports.

d) MolochDAO: Funding Public Goods

- **What It Is:**
  MolochDAO is a grant-making DAO that funds Ethereum-based public goods.
- **How It Works:**
  - Members contribute funds to a shared pool and vote on grant proposals.
  - Decisions are executed transparently through smart contracts.

....

- **Impact:**
  MolochDAO shows how DAOs can address collective needs and support innovation.

Benefits of DAOs in Community Economies

- **Inclusivity:** Anyone with an internet connection can join and contribute.
- **Trustless Collaboration:** Members don't need to trust each other; the rules are enforced by code.
- **Global Reach:** DAOs operate without geographical or political boundaries.
- **Resilience:** Decentralized structures are less vulnerable to corruption or failure.

Challenges Facing DAOs

- **Coordination Issues:** Reaching consensus in large groups can be slow and complex.
- **Regulatory Uncertainty:** Many jurisdictions lack clear legal frameworks for DAOs.
- **Technical Risks:** Smart contract bugs or exploits can jeopardize funds and operations.
- **Participation Gaps:** Not all members actively engage, which can centralize influence among a few.

Opportunities for DAOs in the Future

- **Crowdfunding Innovation:** DAOs can fund startups, art projects and social movements without traditional gatekeepers.
- **Decentralized Workforces:** Teams of freelancers can collaborate through DAOs, with payments and governance automated on-chain.
- **Local and Global Governance:** Communities can self-organize to manage shared resources or advocate for change.
- **Shared Ownership Models:** DAOs can enable fractional ownership of real-world assets, from real estate to renewable energy projects.

DAOs represent a paradigm shift in how communities organize and create value. By decentralizing governance and aligning incentives, they empower individuals to collaborate and share in collective success. Whether funding innovation, owning assets or pursuing cultural goals, DAOs are unlocking new possibilities for global cooperation.

In the next section, we'll delve into **use cases for personal economies**, exploring how individuals can leverage Web3 tools to create value and achieve financial independence.

Local and Global Initiatives

The advent of Web3 and blockchain technology has paved the way for innovative community-driven initiatives that address challenges at both local and global levels. These initiatives harness decentralized tools to empower communities, improve resource allocation and foster collaboration across borders.

Local Initiatives: Empowering Grassroots Communities

Blockchain technology provides tools to solve unique challenges faced by local communities. From transparent funding to fair resource distribution, these solutions strengthen trust and accountability.

a) Grassroots Fundraising and Transparency

Example: GiveDirectly (Blockchain Donations)

What It Is:
GiveDirectly uses blockchain to distribute unconditional cash transfers to people in need in developing countries.

How It Works:

Donors fund wallets and funds are transferred directly to beneficiaries without intermediaries.

Blockchain ensures every transaction is traceable and transparent.

Impact:
Increases trust in charitable donations and ensures funds are used effectively.

b) Local Currencies on Blockchain

Example: Sarafu Network (Kenya)

What It Is:
A blockchain-based local currency system that helps small communities exchange goods and services without relying on national currency.

How It Works:

Residents use Sarafu tokens as a medium of exchange for everyday transactions.

Blockchain ensures transparency and prevents double-spending.

Impact:
Enables financial inclusion and empowers communities to sustain their economies during crises.

c) Transparent Land Registries

Example: Bitland (Ghana)

What It Is:
Bitland digitizes land ownership records on a blockchain to reduce corruption and fraud in land transactions.

How It Works:

Landowners register their property on the blockchain for secure, tamper-proof documentation.

Smart contracts facilitate dispute resolution.

Impact:
Protects land rights, particularly for marginalized groups and builds trust in property transactions.

Global Initiatives: Bridging Borders with Blockchain

Blockchain has enabled global collaboration by creating shared frameworks for solving international challenges, from financial inclusion to environmental sustainability.

a) Universal Basic Income (UBI) via Blockchain

Example: GoodDollar

What It Is:
GoodDollar is a global initiative providing free daily cryptocurrency to anyone as a form of UBI.

How It Works:

Wealthier participants stake funds in DeFi protocols, generating interest used to fund UBI payouts.

Participants claim daily payouts in GoodDollar tokens, which can be exchanged or used within the ecosystem.

Impact:
Promotes financial inclusion and provides a safety net for underserved populations.

b) Decentralized Climate Action

Example: KlimaDAO

What It Is:
KlimaDAO uses blockchain to promote carbon offsetting by tokenizing carbon credits.

How It Works:

Individuals and companies purchase tokenized carbon credits through KlimaDAO.

The DAO ensures the credits are retired, effectively reducing carbon emissions.

Impact:
Increases transparency in carbon markets and incentivizes participation in climate action.

c) Global Financial Inclusion

Example: Stellar Network

What It Is:
Stellar connects financial institutions, enabling cross-border payments and remittances at low costs.

How It Works:

Users send digital assets (e.g., Stellar Lumens or stablecoins) that can be converted into local currencies.

Transactions are completed within seconds, bypassing traditional banking systems.

Impact:
Helps underserved populations access affordable financial services, particularly in regions with weak banking infrastructure.

Key Features of Blockchain for Community Initiatives

- **Transparency:** Ensures all participants can verify transactions and contributions.
- **Inclusion:** Reduces barriers to entry, allowing participation regardless of location or socioeconomic status.
- **Efficiency:** Automates processes, reducing overhead costs and delays.
- **Immutability:** Creates tamper-proof records, building trust in systems.

Challenges of Implementing Blockchain for Community Initiatives

- **Education and Awareness:** Many communities lack knowledge of blockchain and its benefits.
- **Access to Technology:** Reliable internet and devices are required to participate in blockchain ecosystems.
- **Regulatory Hurdles:** Legal uncertainty can hinder the adoption of blockchain-based solutions.
- **Scalability:** Large-scale adoption may strain blockchain networks, leading to high transaction fees.

Opportunities for Scaling Local and Global Initiatives

- **Bridging the Digital Divide:** Expand access to blockchain education and tools in underserved areas.

- **Public-Private Partnerships:** Collaborate with governments and NGOs to implement blockchain-based solutions for social impact.
- **Layer 2 Scaling Solutions:** Use platforms like Polygon and Arbitrum to reduce costs and increase efficiency.
- **Token Incentives:** Reward participation in initiatives with tokens that hold real-world value.

Blockchain technology is reshaping local and global economies, providing tools for transparency, inclusion and collaboration. By empowering communities to take control of their resources and participate in global networks, blockchain is building a more equitable future.

In the next section, we'll explore **personal economies** and how individuals can leverage blockchain to achieve autonomy and financial empowerment.

Financial Inclusion through Web3

Impact on Unbanked and Underbanked Populations

Globally, over 1.4 billion adults remain unbanked, lacking access to traditional financial services such as savings accounts, loans or insurance. An additional segment, the underbanked, has limited access to financial tools, often relying on expensive alternatives like payday loans or cash remittances. Web3, powered by blockchain technology and decentralized finance (DeFi), is breaking these barriers, offering affordable, accessible and inclusive financial solutions.

The Challenges Faced by the Unbanked and Underbanked

- **High Costs:** Traditional banking services often require high fees, especially for cross-border remittances or small transactions.
- **Lack of Documentation:** Millions lack the necessary identification documents required to open a bank account.
- **Geographic Barriers:** Rural areas often lack physical banking infrastructure.
- **Distrust in Banks:** In some regions, historical misuse of funds or financial instability has eroded trust in banks.

Web3 solutions address these challenges by providing decentralized, trustless systems that operate on transparent, programmable blockchains.

How Web3 Empowers the Unbanked and Underbanked

a) Digital Wallets for Global Access

Web3 wallets like MetaMask, Trust Wallet and Celo provide free access to financial systems. Unlike traditional banks, these wallets don't require identification, allowing anyone with a smartphone and internet connection to participate.

Example:

Celo: A blockchain network designed for mobile users, Celo enables easy wallet access and facilitates peer-to-peer payments using stablecoins pegged to local currencies.

Impact:
Communities in Africa and South America use Celo to send and receive money without needing a bank.

b) Remittances Without Borders

Web3 drastically reduces the cost and time for cross-border remittances by bypassing intermediaries.

Example:

Stellar Network: Stellar enables cheap, fast remittances by allowing users to transfer digital assets that are instantly converted into local currencies.

Impact:
Workers in the Philippines and India use Stellar-based apps to send money to their families at a fraction of the cost of traditional services like Western Union.

c) Access to Savings and Lending via DeFi

Decentralized finance platforms allow users to earn interest on savings or borrow funds without requiring credit checks or intermediaries.

Example:

Compound and Aave: These DeFi platforms let users deposit cryptocurrencies and earn interest or take out loans collateralized by their assets.

Impact:
Farmers in Kenya are using crypto-based loans to buy seeds and equipment without relying on traditional banks.

Real-World Success Stories

a) Moeda Seeds (Brazil)

- **What It Is:**
  A blockchain-based microfinance platform supporting small businesses and cooperatives.
- **How It Works:**
  - Entrepreneurs in underserved areas apply for loans funded by global investors through Moeda.
  - Blockchain tracks every transaction, ensuring transparency and accountability.
- **Impact:**
  Farmers and artisans in Brazil now have access to affordable financing, enabling them to grow their businesses sustainably.

b) BitPesa (Africa)

- **What It Is:**
  BitPesa is a blockchain-based payment platform that facilitates cross-border trade and remittances in Africa.
- **How It Works:**
  - Users can send payments in Bitcoin, which is then converted into local currencies.
  - The service bypasses traditional banking fees and delays.
- **Impact:**
  SMEs in Nigeria and Kenya use BitPesa to pay international suppliers, reducing costs and increasing efficiency.

c) Bancor Network and Local Currencies (Kenya)

- **What It Is:**
  Bancor supports community currencies like Sarafu in Kenya, enabling people to transact even without national currency.
- **How It Works:**
  - Community members earn and spend Sarafu tokens for goods and services.
  - Bancor provides liquidity, ensuring that Sarafu can be exchanged for other assets when needed.
- **Impact:**
  During economic downturns, Sarafu has enabled local trade and prevented economic stagnation in rural areas.

Benefits of Web3 for Financial Inclusion

- **Cost Efficiency:** Web3 eliminates intermediaries, reducing fees for transactions and remittances.

- **Accessibility:** Decentralized systems are open to anyone with internet access, regardless of location or socioeconomic status.
- **Transparency:** Blockchain provides an immutable record of transactions, fostering trust among users.
- **Self-Sovereignty:** Users retain full control over their funds and data, reducing reliance on third parties.

Challenges to Overcome

- **Technological Barriers:** Limited access to smartphones, reliable internet or energy in some regions.
- **Education Gap:** Many users lack knowledge of blockchain or how to use Web3 tools effectively.
- **Volatility:** Cryptocurrencies can be highly volatile, making them less practical for everyday use in some cases.
- **Regulatory Concerns:** Governments may restrict or ban crypto-related activities, citing concerns over fraud or tax evasion.

The Future of Web3 and Financial Inclusion

- **Stablecoins for Everyday Use:** Pegged to fiat currencies, stablecoins provide a practical solution for daily transactions without volatility concerns.
- **Layer 2 Solutions:** Platforms like Polygon and Optimism offer low-cost transactions, making Web3 tools affordable for all.
- **Integration with Existing Systems:** Partnerships between Web3 platforms and local governments or

NGOs can expand access to underserved populations.
- **Localized Solutions:** Developing blockchain tools tailored to specific regions or needs, such as rural banking or agriculture financing.

Web3 has the potential to transform the lives of the unbanked and underbanked by providing access to affordable, efficient and transparent financial tools. By bypassing traditional barriers and enabling global participation, blockchain technology is creating a more inclusive financial ecosystem.

In the next section, we'll explore how **Web3 fosters innovation in industries like healthcare, education and sustainability**, driving impact beyond the financial sector.

Part IV: Challenges and Risks

Regulatory Hurdles

Navigating the Legal Landscape

As blockchain technology and Web3 applications grow, they are challenging traditional regulatory frameworks. Governments worldwide are grappling with how to manage the risks and opportunities posed by decentralized systems. For individuals and organizations in the Web3 ecosystem, navigating this legal uncertainty is a critical step toward sustainable growth.

Why Regulation Matters

- **Consumer Protection:** Prevents fraud, scams and misuse of funds.
- **Market Stability:** Ensures fair practices and reduces risks associated with volatility.
- **Preventing Illicit Activity:** Helps combat money laundering, tax evasion and financing of illegal operations.

However, excessive or unclear regulations can stifle innovation and exclude communities that could benefit most from decentralized solutions.

Key Regulatory Challenges

a) Defining Digital Assets

Governments struggle to classify cryptocurrencies and tokens:

- Are they securities, commodities or currencies?
- Classification impacts how they are taxed, traded and regulated.

Example:

In the U.S., the Securities and Exchange Commission (SEC) considers some tokens securities, subjecting them to strict compliance rules. This has created uncertainty for projects like Ripple's XRP, which faced a legal battle over its classification.

b) Cross-Border Transactions

Web3 operates globally, but regulations are local.

- Different jurisdictions impose conflicting rules, making compliance complex.
- Decentralized platforms without a central entity face challenges in adhering to jurisdictional laws.

Example:

Binance, the largest cryptocurrency exchange, has faced regulatory scrutiny in multiple countries, including the U.S., UK and Japan, over compliance with local laws.

c) Taxation of Digital Assets

Tax authorities seek to capture revenue from crypto transactions, but inconsistent rules confuse users.

- How are staking rewards, airdrops or NFT sales taxed?
- What happens if tokens lose value after a taxable event?

Example:

....

In India, a flat 30% tax on crypto gains and a 1% tax on every transaction have deterred small investors and traders.

d) Privacy vs. Compliance

Blockchain's transparency conflicts with privacy laws, like the EU's General Data Protection Regulation (GDPR).

- Public ledgers make transactions visible, but GDPR demands the "right to be forgotten."
- Balancing privacy with anti-money laundering (AML) rules adds complexity.

Example:

Tornado Cash, a privacy tool on Ethereum, was sanctioned by the U.S. government for allegedly facilitating money laundering, sparking debate over the legality of privacy-focused tools.

Strategies for Navigating the Legal Landscape

a) Proactive Compliance

Engage with regulators early and ensure transparency.

- Conduct thorough legal reviews of tokenomics and operations.
- Register where required and adhere to know-your-customer (KYC) and anti-money laundering (AML) guidelines.

Example:

Coinbase works closely with U.S. regulators to maintain compliance, making it a trusted platform despite regulatory challenges.

b) Decentralization as a Shield

Decentralized platforms with no single point of control can mitigate regulatory risks. However, full decentralization can complicate user protection and compliance.

Example:

Uniswap, a decentralized exchange, operates without a central authority but faces scrutiny for facilitating unregulated token trading.

c) Use of Regulatory Sandboxes

Some jurisdictions offer sandboxes where Web3 projects can operate under relaxed rules to test their models.

Example:

The UAE launched a crypto sandbox to attract blockchain startups while maintaining oversight.

d) Educating Users

Projects should provide clear guidance on legal implications, including tax obligations and compliance with local laws.

Jurisdictional Approaches to Web3 Regulation

a) Crypto-Friendly Jurisdictions

Some countries embrace blockchain innovation with clear, supportive laws:

- **Switzerland (Crypto Valley):** Provides a regulatory framework for ICOs and token-based projects.
- **Singapore:** Implements balanced regulations, fostering innovation while ensuring compliance.

b) Restrictive Jurisdictions

Other countries have banned or severely restricted crypto use:

- **China:** Outlawed crypto trading and mining, though blockchain development is encouraged.
- **India:** Imposed high taxes, discouraging active participation.

c) Collaborative Models

Regional bodies like the European Union are developing unified frameworks, such as the Markets in Crypto-Assets (MiCA) regulation, to streamline rules across member states.

Opportunities in Regulatory Challenges

Despite the hurdles, regulation offers opportunities:

- **Enhanced Credibility:** Clear rules build trust with institutional investors and traditional businesses.
- **Wider Adoption:** Consumers feel safer using regulated platforms, driving mainstream adoption.
- **Market Maturity:** Effective regulation fosters stability and growth, benefiting the entire ecosystem.

Navigating the legal landscape in Web3 is complex but crucial for long-term success. By understanding regulatory frameworks and proactively addressing compliance issues, Web3 projects can thrive while building trust with users and governments.

In the next section, we'll examine **technological challenges** in scaling Web3, such as improving speed, cost-efficiency and user experience, to meet growing demands.

Balancing Innovation and Compliance

Blockchain technology and Web3 applications are driving innovation at an unprecedented pace, reshaping industries from finance to healthcare. However, this rapid growth often collides with regulatory frameworks designed for traditional, centralized systems. Balancing innovation and compliance is essential to ensure both the growth of the Web3 ecosystem and the protection of consumers and markets.

The Tension Between Innovation and Regulation

Regulators aim to maintain financial stability, prevent fraud and enforce fair practices. At the same time, overly strict or outdated regulations can stifle innovation and deter investment.

Example:

The SEC's lawsuit against Ripple Labs over XRP's status as a security created uncertainty for blockchain developers and investors in the U.S., slowing innovation in the sector.

In contrast, countries like Switzerland have established clear, flexible regulations, attracting blockchain startups to its "Crypto Valley."

Innovation-Friendly Approaches

Some jurisdictions have taken proactive steps to foster innovation while maintaining oversight, creating win-win scenarios for regulators and innovators.

a) Regulatory Sandboxes

These controlled environments allow blockchain projects to operate under relaxed regulations while authorities monitor their impact.

Example:

UAE's Crypto Sandbox: Encourages startups to test blockchain solutions, offering guidance without full regulatory enforcement.

Impact: Startups like WadzPay and BitOasis have scaled operations while ensuring compliance, contributing to the UAE's fintech ecosystem.

b) Principle-Based Regulation

Instead of rigid rules, some countries use principles to guide blockchain innovation, allowing flexibility as technology evolves.

Example:

The UK's Financial Conduct Authority (FCA) employs principle-based regulation for crypto projects, focusing on outcomes like transparency and fairness rather than prescribing specific methods.

Impact: This approach has attracted companies like Revolut, which integrates crypto services under a flexible framework.

The Risks of Over-Regulation

a) Stifling Small Innovators

Heavy compliance requirements often impose high costs, favoring large corporations over small startups.

Example:

India's 30% tax on crypto profits and 1% transaction tax have significantly reduced trading volumes and driven startups to relocate to crypto-friendly jurisdictions like Dubai.

b) Innovation Exodus

Overly restrictive environments risk pushing talent and investment to countries with clearer or more favorable regulations.

Example:

China banned crypto trading and mining in 2021, but many Chinese blockchain developers moved to Singapore and the U.S., strengthening those markets instead.

The Risks of Under-Regulation

While over-regulation is a threat, insufficient oversight can lead to risks that undermine the entire ecosystem:

a) Consumer Harm

Without protections, scams and fraud can proliferate.

Example:

The collapse of Terra's algorithmic stablecoin (UST) and Luna token in 2022 wiped out billions of dollars in value, affecting millions of retail investors worldwide.

b) Systemic Risks

Unchecked innovation can lead to systemic risks, such as market manipulation or financial instability.

Example:

The 2022 bankruptcy of FTX highlighted the need for clearer regulations on exchanges and custodians.

Strategies for Balancing Innovation and Compliance

a) Collaborative Regulation

Regulators and innovators must engage in dialogue to create frameworks that foster innovation while protecting users.

Example:

MiCA (Markets in Crypto-Assets): The EU developed MiCA regulations after consulting with blockchain companies, ensuring rules support innovation while addressing risks.

Impact: MiCA provides clarity for businesses, reducing compliance uncertainty and fostering innovation in Europe.

b) Adapting Existing Laws

Rather than creating entirely new laws, regulators can adapt existing ones to address blockchain-specific issues.

Example:

Switzerland applies existing financial laws to crypto projects while creating specific guidelines for token sales.

....

Impact: This approach simplifies compliance and has made Switzerland a global hub for blockchain innovation.

c) Encouraging Self-Regulation

Industry-driven standards can complement government oversight.

Example:

The Crypto Rating Council (CRC), formed by major exchanges like Coinbase and Kraken, evaluates tokens to determine if they resemble securities, offering transparency for developers and investors.

Examples of Successful Balancing Acts

a) Singapore's Balanced Approach

- **Regulatory Model:**
    - Encourages blockchain innovation while enforcing strict anti-money laundering (AML) and know-your-customer (KYC) rules.
- **Impact:**
    - Singapore is home to blockchain projects like VeChain and Decentralized Information Asset (DIA), thriving in a secure yet innovation-friendly environment.

b) Estonia's Digital Transformation

- **Regulatory Model:**

- **Impact:**
    - Embraces blockchain for government services while ensuring crypto businesses follow licensing rules.
    - Estonia has become a leader in blockchain-based e-governance, inspiring global adoption of digital identities.

---

7. The Future of Balanced Regulation

- **Global Coordination:**
  Regulators must collaborate internationally to address the borderless nature of Web3.
- **Technology-Driven Compliance:**
  Blockchain itself can support compliance through smart contracts and transparent record-keeping, reducing regulatory burdens.
- **Iterative Approaches:**
  Regulations must evolve with the technology, embracing iterative improvements rather than rigid, one-time frameworks.

Balancing innovation and compliance in Web3 is not an easy task, but it is crucial for long-term success. By fostering dialogue, adopting flexible frameworks and leveraging blockchain's inherent transparency, regulators and innovators can create an environment where innovation thrives while protecting users and markets.

In the next section, we'll discuss **technological challenges**, including scalability, energy consumption and user adoption, as Web3 continues to grow.

Security and Scalability Concerns

Risks in Smart Contracts and Tokenomics

While blockchain technology promises security and decentralization, it is not immune to vulnerabilities. The complexity of smart contracts and tokenomics introduces risks that, if unaddressed, can lead to significant financial losses and damage to trust in the Web3 ecosystem.

Risks in Smart Contracts

Smart contracts are self-executing agreements with code running on the blockchain. They are essential for enabling decentralized applications (dApps) and programmable money, but they come with inherent risks.

a) Vulnerable Code

Smart contracts are only as secure as their code. A single bug or oversight can be exploited.

Example:

The DAO Hack (2016):
A vulnerability in the smart contract code of The DAO (a decentralized autonomous organization) allowed an attacker to drain $60 million in Ether. This incident led to a hard fork of the Ethereum blockchain, splitting it into Ethereum (ETH) and Ethereum Classic (ETC).

b) Over-Reliance on Oracles

Smart contracts often rely on external data sources (oracles) to execute. If an oracle provides false or malicious data, it can compromise the contract.

Example:

In 2020, an attacker manipulated the price feed of an oracle to exploit a DeFi protocol, bZx, resulting in a loss of $8 million.

c) Reentrancy Attacks

These occur when a malicious contract repeatedly calls a vulnerable function before it resolves, draining funds.

Example:

The dForce Hack (2020):
The dForce protocol lost $25 million due to a reentrancy attack. The funds were later returned by the hacker, but the incident highlighted the importance of secure coding practices.

d) Lack of Auditing

Some projects skip thorough code audits due to cost or time constraints, increasing vulnerability.

Risks in Tokenomics

The design of a token's economics (tokenomics) directly impacts its sustainability and value. Poorly designed tokenomics can result in market manipulation, instability or even collapse.

a) Pump-and-Dump Schemes

Tokens with low liquidity and weak governance are susceptible to pump-and-dump schemes, where prices are artificially inflated and then sold off, leaving other investors with worthless tokens.

Example:

In 2021, the **Squid Game Token** soared by over 230,000% before the anonymous creators pulled liquidity, effectively scamming investors out of $3 million.

b) Inflationary Models

Tokens with unlimited supply or poorly managed inflation can lose value rapidly, discouraging long-term adoption.

Example:

Dogecoin's inflationary tokenomics limits its utility as a store of value, leading to high volatility.

c) Misaligned Incentives

If token rewards are distributed without aligning stakeholders' long-term interests, it can lead to unsustainable ecosystems.

Example:

Some DeFi platforms offer high yield farming rewards, attracting speculators rather than long-term users, resulting in market crashes when incentives dry up.

d) Governance Risks

In decentralized systems, governance tokens allow holders to vote on decisions. If governance is concentrated in a few hands, it undermines decentralization and opens doors to manipulation.

Example:

In 2022, a whale holding a significant portion of governance tokens on Solend, a Solana-based lending platform, nearly caused a liquidation crisis due to centralized decision-making power.

Mitigating Security and Tokenomics Risks

a) Code Audits and Bug Bounties

- Conduct rigorous audits with trusted firms like CertiK, ConsenSys Diligence or Trail of Bits.
- Offer bug bounties to incentivize ethical hackers to identify vulnerabilities.

Example:

Compound Finance regularly undergoes audits and hosts bug bounty programs, ensuring its smart contracts remain secure.

b) Implementing Insurance Protocols

DeFi insurance platforms like Nexus Mutual and InsurAce offer coverage against smart contract failures and hacks.

Example:

After the Cream Finance hack in 2021, users insured through Nexus Mutual were compensated for their losses.

c) Decentralized Oracle Solutions

Using decentralized oracles like Chainlink reduces reliance on a single data source, mitigating oracle manipulation risks.

Example:

Aave, a DeFi protocol, uses Chainlink oracles for price feeds to ensure data reliability.

d) Thoughtful Token Design

- Use capped supply models or burn mechanisms to prevent over-inflation.
- Design incentives to reward long-term participation rather than speculation.

Example:

Ethereum 2.0 introduced a staking mechanism to reward participants for securing the network, aligning incentives with the network's health.

e) Distributed Governance

Adopt governance models that prevent token concentration and encourage active, diverse participation.

Example:

MakerDAO distributes governance through MKR token holders, requiring broad consensus for major changes.

The Road Ahead

To build trust and scale adoption, the Web3 ecosystem must address security and tokenomics risks effectively.

- **Innovation in Smart Contracts:** Developers are exploring formal verification methods to mathematically prove a contract's security.
- **Improved Tokenomics Models:** Research into game theory and behavioral economics can lead to more robust designs that align stakeholder interests.
- **Collaborative Efforts:** Industry-wide initiatives like the OpenZeppelin library for secure contracts help standardize best practices.

Security and tokenomics risks are critical challenges for Web3, but they are not insurmountable. By adopting rigorous security practices, thoughtful token design and decentralized governance, the ecosystem can build resilience and trust. These efforts will lay the foundation for a more secure and scalable blockchain future, paving the way for mass adoption.

In the next section, we will explore **scalability challenges**, focusing on how blockchain networks can meet the demands of a growing user base without compromising speed or cost.

Solutions Like Auditing and Layer 2 Tech

As blockchain adoption grows, addressing security vulnerabilities and scalability limitations becomes paramount. Auditing practices and Layer 2 technologies are two critical solutions to enhance the security and performance of blockchain networks while maintaining their decentralized ethos.

Security Solutions: Smart Contract Auditing

Auditing is the process of thoroughly reviewing smart contract code to identify vulnerabilities before deployment. With billions of dollars locked in decentralized applications (dApps), robust auditing practices are essential to prevent exploits.

a) Comprehensive Audits

Professional auditing firms analyze smart contract logic, testing for vulnerabilities like reentrancy, integer overflows or improper access controls.

Example:

Compound Finance:
Conducts frequent audits by firms like OpenZeppelin and CertiK to secure its lending protocols, minimizing risks for users.

Uniswap:
Undergoes multiple audits for each major upgrade, ensuring the integrity of its decentralized exchange contracts.

b) Automated Testing Tools

Tools like MythX, Slither and Echidna automatically scan smart contracts for common vulnerabilities.

Example:

Developers of SushiSwap used Slither during its launch to detect early-stage issues, improving contract robustness before deployment.

c) Bug Bounties

Platforms incentivize ethical hackers to find and report vulnerabilities.

Example:

Immunefi:
Hosts bounty programs for projects like MakerDAO and Synthetix, rewarding hackers with millions for uncovering critical bugs.

Scalability Solutions: Layer 2 Technologies

Scalability is a major bottleneck for blockchain networks, especially those with high traffic, like Ethereum. Layer 2 (L2) technologies aim to increase transaction throughput and reduce fees without compromising security.

a) What Are Layer 2 Solutions?

Layer 2 solutions operate atop the main blockchain (Layer 1) to process transactions off-chain or in batches, reducing the load on the base layer.

Types of Layer 2 Technologies

a) Rollups

Rollups bundle multiple transactions into a single batch, which is processed off-chain and then recorded on-chain for security.

Optimistic Rollups: Assume transactions are valid unless proven otherwise.

Example:

Optimism and Arbitrum: Reduce Ethereum gas fees while maintaining compatibility with existing smart contracts. Projects like Uniswap and Aave have adopted these solutions to offer users lower costs.

ZK (Zero-Knowledge) Rollups: Use cryptographic proofs to verify transactions off-chain before submitting them on-chain.

Example:

zkSync: A ZK-rollup platform enabling near-instant transactions for Ethereum, supporting dApps like Gitcoin for cost-effective donations.

b) Sidechains

Independent blockchains linked to the main chain, designed for scalability and specific use cases.

Example:

Polygon: A popular sidechain for Ethereum that supports dApps like OpenSea and Aave. By offloading transactions, Polygon offers lower fees and faster processing times.

c) Payment Channels

Peer-to-peer channels allow users to conduct multiple transactions off-chain and settle the final state on-chain.

Example:

Lightning Network (Bitcoin): Enables instant, low-cost transactions for Bitcoin, making it practical for microtransactions and remittances.

d) State Channels

Enable participants to execute smart contract transactions off-chain while maintaining security guarantees.

Example:

Raiden Network: Ethereum's state channel solution for fast and scalable token transfers.

Benefits of Layer 2 Solutions

a) Cost Reduction

By offloading transactions from the main chain, L2 solutions significantly reduce gas fees.

Example:

Ethereum transactions on Arbitrum or Optimism cost a fraction of Layer 1 fees, enhancing accessibility for users.

b) Faster Transactions

By reducing congestion on the main chain, L2 solutions enable near-instant transaction confirmations.

Example:

Lightning Network processes payments in seconds, addressing Bitcoin's scalability issues.

c) Broader Accessibility

Lower costs and faster speeds make blockchain more accessible to users in developing regions.

Example:

zkSync and Polygon have been instrumental in supporting affordable blockchain-based applications in financial inclusion projects.

Combining Auditing and L2 for a Secure, Scalable Future

a) Secure, Scalable dApps

dApps that integrate L2 solutions and undergo rigorous audits offer better performance and reduced risk.

Example:

SushiSwap on Arbitrum: Combines scalability with security measures, delivering an efficient and reliable DeFi experience.

b) Enhanced Developer Ecosystems

By providing audited templates and L2 integration toolkits, blockchain platforms can attract developers to build scalable and secure applications.

Example:

OpenZeppelin's Contracts Library: Offers pre-audited smart contract templates, reducing developer workload and increasing security.

c) Future-Proofing Web3

As blockchain adoption grows, combining Layer 2 scalability with rigorous security practices will ensure the Web3 ecosystem remains resilient and accessible.

Auditing practices address vulnerabilities, ensuring that smart contracts are robust and reliable. Layer 2 technologies solve scalability challenges, making blockchain networks faster and more cost-effective. Together, these solutions form the backbone of a secure and scalable Web3 ecosystem, paving the way for mass adoption.

In the next section, we'll explore **user adoption challenges** and how improving education and user experience can drive Web3 growth.

Market Risks and Adoption Barriers

Speculation vs. Utility

The cryptocurrency and Web3 ecosystem is often divided between speculative activity and real-world utility. Speculation brings attention, liquidity and early growth to the industry. However, it can overshadow or even hinder projects focused on providing meaningful utility. Understanding this dynamic is critical for the long-term sustainability of the space.

The Role of Speculation

Speculation refers to buying and selling assets with the expectation of profit from price changes, often without regard to the intrinsic value or utility of the asset.

a) Rapid Growth Fueled by Speculation

Speculation has been a significant driver of cryptocurrency adoption, drawing in investors and traders who hope to capitalize on price volatility.

Example:

Dogecoin: A meme cryptocurrency with limited technical features. It gained immense popularity in 2021 due to social media hype, celebrity endorsements and speculative trading, reaching a market cap of over $88 billion at its peak.

b) Risks of Over-Speculation

Markets dominated by speculation often experience:

- **Volatility:** Prices can rise or fall sharply, creating uncertainty for long-term investors.
- **Bubbles:** Speculative hype can inflate asset values far beyond their utility. When the bubble bursts, it can lead to financial losses and distrust in the ecosystem.

Example:

2017 ICO Bubble: Initial Coin Offerings (ICOs) raised billions, with many projects failing to deliver on promises, causing a market crash and skepticism about crypto projects.

The Power of Utility

Utility refers to the practical uses of cryptocurrencies or tokens in solving real-world problems, such as enabling transactions, providing governance or accessing services. Projects with clear utility are more likely to sustain long-term value.

a) Utility-Driven Success Stories

Ethereum (ETH): Known for its ability to execute smart contracts, Ethereum powers decentralized finance (DeFi), NFTs and decentralized applications (dApps). Its widespread utility ensures ongoing demand for ETH.

Chainlink (LINK): A decentralized oracle network that connects blockchain smart contracts to real-world data, enabling functionalities like insurance payouts and financial services.

b) Community and Ecosystem Growth

Utility-focused projects often foster strong communities, which are essential for long-term success.

Example:

Helium (HNT): Enables individuals to build a decentralized IoT network by running hotspots. The HNT token rewards participants, creating a user-driven ecosystem with real-world applications.

Striking a Balance: Speculation as a Catalyst

Speculation isn't inherently bad - it can serve as a gateway to adoption by generating initial interest. However, it must eventually give way to utility for sustainable growth.

a) Speculation Sparks Interest

- **Bitcoin's Rise:** Initially driven by speculative trading, Bitcoin gained recognition as "digital gold" and a hedge against inflation, transitioning to a utility-focused narrative.

b) The Shift Toward Utility

Projects need to demonstrate tangible benefits to attract users and investors seeking long-term value.

Challenges in Balancing Speculation and Utility

a) Overhyped Projects

Hype-driven projects with little or no utility may overshadow genuinely impactful solutions.

Example:

In 2022, many NFT collections surged in value due to speculation but lacked functionality, leading to significant price declines when market enthusiasm waned.

b) Misaligned Incentives

Speculators prioritize short-term gains, while utility-focused participants invest in long-term impact. This misalignment can create friction within communities.

Strategies to Promote Utility

a) Real-World Use Cases

Projects should focus on clear and measurable applications.

Example:

Aave (AAVE): A decentralized lending platform that allows users to borrow assets without intermediaries. Its token has governance and staking utility, aligning with its core purpose.

b) Transparent Tokenomics

Token supply and demand mechanisms should encourage sustainable growth.

Example:

Polygon (MATIC): Used for paying transaction fees and staking on the network. Its utility directly supports the functionality of the Polygon ecosystem.

c) Educating Investors

Providing resources to help users understand the technology can reduce reliance on speculation.

Example:

CoinGecko's Resources: Offers educational content on blockchain projects, helping users evaluate them based on utility instead of hype.

Moving Forward: The Importance of Balance

To achieve mainstream adoption, the crypto industry must balance speculation with utility. Speculation can bring attention and funding, but long-term success depends on building systems that solve real problems and create lasting value.

Key Takeaway:

Utility-driven innovation ensures that Web3 technologies remain relevant and impactful beyond market trends. Speculation may come and go, but utility builds ecosystems that thrive.

In the next section, we'll explore how **user experience and accessibility** can further accelerate the adoption of Web3 technologies.

Overcoming Adoption Challenges

While Web3 and blockchain technologies offer revolutionary potential, their widespread adoption faces significant challenges. These include technological complexity, usability barriers and a lack of public trust. Overcoming these hurdles is essential to making Web3 accessible and meaningful to individuals and communities worldwide.

Understanding Adoption Challenges

a) Complexity of Blockchain Technology

Blockchain concepts like smart contracts, private keys and decentralized networks can be intimidating to non-technical users. The steep learning curve discourages many from exploring Web3 applications.

Example:

Wallets like **MetaMask** require users to manage private keys and seed phrases, which can be confusing for first-time users. Mistakes, such as losing a seed phrase, can result in irreversible loss of funds.

b) Poor User Experience (UX)

Early blockchain applications often lack intuitive design, making them difficult for mainstream users to navigate.

Example:

Decentralized exchanges (DEXs) like **Uniswap** offer powerful features but may confuse new users unfamiliar with terms like "slippage" or how to connect a wallet.

c) Limited Trust and Misconceptions

Blockchain's association with scams, hacks and volatility creates skepticism. Many people perceive it as risky or irrelevant to their daily lives.

Example:

News of exchange collapses, such as the **FTX bankruptcy**, erodes public trust and deters potential adopters.

d) Infrastructure Gaps

In regions with limited internet access or outdated hardware, accessing blockchain networks and Web3 applications can be challenging.

Example:

High transaction fees on Ethereum during peak usage make it unaffordable for users in developing countries to participate in DeFi or mint NFTs.

Strategies for Overcoming Adoption Challenges

a) Simplifying User Onboarding

Making blockchain technology more accessible through intuitive interfaces and user-friendly experiences is critical.

Examples:

Coinbase Wallet: A beginner-friendly app that simplifies wallet creation and management, allowing users to explore DeFi and NFTs with fewer barriers.

Web3Auth: Eliminates seed phrases by enabling login through social media accounts, bridging the gap between traditional and blockchain systems.

b) Enhancing Education and Awareness

Educating users about blockchain's benefits and real-world applications can help demystify the technology.

Examples:

Binance Academy: Provides free courses and resources to teach blockchain fundamentals.

Scholareum: Offers crypto education, scholarships and hands-on experience for underrepresented communities.

c) Building Trust with Regulation and Transparency

Clear regulations and transparent operations can reduce scams and increase confidence in blockchain ecosystems.

Examples:

Countries like **El Salvador** adopting Bitcoin as legal tender have introduced regulatory frameworks to ensure its safe use.

CertiK: A blockchain security company that audits smart contracts to ensure their reliability, reducing risks for users.

d) Addressing Scalability and Cost Issues

Layer 2 solutions and alternative blockchains are critical for improving transaction speeds and reducing costs.

Examples:

Polygon: Provides a scalable platform for Ethereum-based applications, drastically reducing fees and enabling smoother transactions.

Solana: Known for high-speed, low-cost transactions, making blockchain more accessible for gaming and NFT platforms.

e) Localized Solutions for Global Challenges

Adapting Web3 technologies to address the unique needs of diverse regions can drive adoption.

Examples:

Celo: A mobile-first blockchain focusing on financial inclusion in developing countries, enabling users to send and receive money using just a phone number.

BitPesa: Uses blockchain to facilitate cross-border payments in Africa, reducing costs and improving efficiency.

The Role of Innovation and Collaboration

a) No-Code Tools for Empowerment

Simplified tools allow individuals and small businesses to create blockchain projects without technical expertise.

Examples:

Zora: A platform enabling creators to mint and sell NFTs without needing programming skills.

Mintable: Offers a straightforward interface for minting NFTs and managing digital assets.

b) Public-Private Partnerships

Collaboration between governments, private enterprises and blockchain developers can drive infrastructure development and regulatory clarity.

Examples:

India's Blockchain Initiatives: The Indian government collaborates with blockchain firms to explore use cases in land registry, identity verification and supply chain management.

World Food Programme: Uses blockchain to distribute aid to refugees securely, ensuring transparency and reducing costs.

Measuring Success

Widespread adoption will depend on addressing the core challenges of accessibility, trust and utility. Metrics such as active wallet users, transaction volume and the number of dApps with real-world applications can indicate progress.

a) Key Indicators of Progress

- Growth in decentralized finance (DeFi) platforms providing accessible loans.
- Increased NFT adoption for purposes beyond art, such as ticketing and memberships.
- The rise of DAOs (Decentralized Autonomous Organizations) that enable communities to collaborate globally.

b) Success Stories

- **Axie Infinity in the Philippines:** Many users earned a living by playing the blockchain-based game during the COVID-19 pandemic, demonstrating how Web3 can provide financial opportunities in challenging times.
- **Ethereum Name Service (ENS):** Simplifies wallet addresses into human-readable names, making blockchain interactions less intimidating.

Overcoming adoption challenges is essential for realizing the full potential of Web3 and blockchain technologies. By focusing on user experience, education, affordability and trust, the industry can make decentralized solutions accessible to a broader audience. As adoption grows, these systems will empower individuals and communities worldwide to participate in the next era of the internet.

In the following section, we'll explore **ethical considerations in Web3**, including data privacy, inclusivity and environmental sustainability.

Part V: The Future of Personal Currencies

Interoperability and the Metaverse

How Personal Currencies Fit into a Connected, Immersive Future

As the concept of the metaverse evolves, it promises to create a seamless digital world where individuals can work, play, shop and socialize. Personal currencies, powered by blockchain technology, have the potential to play a central role in this interconnected, immersive landscape. Through interoperability, these tokens can transcend platform boundaries, enabling fluid economic activity across the metaverse.

What Is Interoperability in Web3?

Interoperability refers to the ability of different blockchain networks, platforms and systems to work together seamlessly. In the context of personal currencies, it means that tokens created on one blockchain or for one specific purpose can be used across multiple platforms, networks or applications.

Examples of Interoperability in Action:

Cross-Chain Bridges: Tools like **Wormhole** and **Polygon Bridge** allow assets to move between blockchain networks like Ethereum, Solana and Binance Smart Chain.

Universal Wallets: Wallets like **MetaMask** and **Trust Wallet** support multiple blockchains, enabling users to interact with various ecosystems without switching platforms.

The Role of Personal Currencies in the Metaverse

In the metaverse, personal currencies represent a new way for individuals and communities to create, exchange and govern value. These currencies are programmable and customizable, enabling diverse use cases.

a) Empowering Digital Identity and Ownership

Personal tokens can reflect an individual's brand, achievements or contributions to the digital world.

Example:

A musician issues a personal token tied to exclusive digital experiences or NFTs in a virtual concert on platforms like **Decentraland** or **The Sandbox**.

b) Seamless Value Exchange Across Platforms

In the metaverse, users might navigate multiple virtual worlds. Personal currencies can ensure that economic activities aren't siloed within individual platforms.

Example:

A designer's token from one platform, like **Voxels**, can be accepted in another, such as **Spatial**, for virtual clothing or furniture sales.

c) Supporting Community Economies

Communities can issue shared tokens to incentivize participation and reward contributions, fostering vibrant digital ecosystems.

Example:

A gaming community uses a token for in-game rewards, governance decisions and real-world merchandise discounts, usable across different games or marketplaces.

Interoperability Challenges and Innovations

While interoperability is vital for the metaverse, achieving it faces technical and conceptual hurdles.

a) Technical Barriers

- **Blockchain Fragmentation:** Many blockchains operate in isolation, making it difficult for tokens or data to move freely.
- **High Costs:** Bridging assets across chains often incurs significant fees, limiting accessibility for smaller transactions.

Innovations Addressing These Barriers:

- **Layer 2 Networks:** Platforms like **Arbitrum** and **Optimism** reduce costs and enable faster transactions, improving cross-platform usability.
- **Cross-Chain Standards:** Protocols like **Polkadot** and **Cosmos** focus on creating interconnected ecosystems, allowing blockchains to communicate and exchange data efficiently.

b) Conceptual Challenges

- **Trust and Security:** Interoperability mechanisms, like cross-chain bridges, are often targets for hacks and exploits.

- **Standardization:** The lack of universally accepted standards for token creation and transfer slows integration across platforms.

Promising Developments:

- **Zero-Knowledge Proofs:** Advanced cryptography ensures secure asset transfers across chains without compromising privacy.
- **NFT Standards:** Standards like **ERC-721** and **ERC-1155** have already enabled interoperable digital assets like NFTs.

The Vision of a Fully Interoperable Metaverse

Imagine a metaverse where personal currencies enable seamless, borderless economic activity.

a) Use Case 1: A Creator Economy Without Borders

- A graphic designer sells virtual art minted as NFTs. Their personal token, tied to their brand, can be redeemed for customized artwork across multiple virtual galleries, such as **OpenSea**, **Rarible** or a bespoke gallery in a metaverse space like **OnCyber**.

b) Use Case 2: Universal Gaming Economies

- A gamer earns tokens in one game, which they can exchange for skins, weapons or upgrades in another game built on a compatible platform. This creates a truly interconnected gaming economy.

Example:

....

Projects like **Enjin** already explore interoperability for in-game assets, allowing players to bring digital items across games and even outside the gaming ecosystem.

c) Use Case 3: Virtual and Physical Integration

- A user can redeem personal tokens earned in the metaverse for real-world goods, services or even equity in their favorite projects.

Benefits of Personal Currencies in the Metaverse

a) Increased Control and Ownership

Users control their own tokens and data, reducing reliance on centralized platforms.

b) Economic Empowerment

Personal tokens allow creators and communities to monetize their contributions directly, bypassing intermediaries.

c) Global Accessibility

Anyone with an internet connection can participate, broadening opportunities for financial inclusion.

The Road Ahead: Collaboration and Innovation

Building an interoperable metaverse requires collaboration among developers, platforms and policymakers. Key steps include:

- Establishing common technical standards for tokens and data exchange.
- Enhancing user experience to make interoperability seamless for non-technical users.
- Ensuring security to protect users and their assets.

Personal currencies are poised to become the backbone of the metaverse's economy, enabling individuals and communities to interact in ways that transcend traditional boundaries. As interoperability improves, these tokens will unlock a future where economic activity flows freely across digital and physical worlds, empowering users to shape their own destinies in this connected, immersive era.

In the next section, we will explore **scalability solutions and their role in building the metaverse of tomorrow.**

AI and Personalized Finance

Role of AI in Managing and Optimizing Personal Currencies

Artificial Intelligence (AI) is transforming the financial landscape, making wealth management smarter, more accessible and highly personalized. In the realm of Web3 and personal currencies, AI can play a pivotal role in helping individuals and communities optimize their tokens, manage risks and maximize value. By combining the power of blockchain with AI's analytical and predictive capabilities, users can create more efficient, automated and user-friendly financial systems.

AI's Role in Personal Currency Management

a) Automated Portfolio Management

AI-powered tools can analyze market trends, token performance and user preferences to optimize personal token portfolios.

Example:

An artist with a personal token can use AI to assess the token's trading activity and adjust supply or utility based on demand. Platforms like **Zerion** use AI to provide real-time insights into DeFi portfolios, which can be adapted for personal tokens.

b) Smart Staking Strategies

AI algorithms can determine the most lucrative staking or yield farming opportunities for a personal or community token, ensuring steady returns without manual effort.

Example:

A DAO can use AI to allocate treasury funds into the most profitable staking protocols on platforms like **Aave** or **Compound**, optimizing returns while minimizing risks.

c) Dynamic Tokenomics

AI can dynamically adjust the parameters of personal or community tokens, such as supply, rewards or governance models, based on market conditions and user behavior.

Example:

A creator's token could automatically increase its rewards for holders during high engagement periods (e.g., a new content release) to boost demand.

AI-Powered Tools for Personal Currencies

a) Predictive Analytics

AI uses historical data and real-time inputs to predict token performance, helping individuals and communities make informed decisions.

Example:

Platforms like **Token Metrics** analyze crypto trends and provide AI-driven insights that can guide personal currency holders in optimizing their token's utility or distribution strategies.

b) Personal Financial Assistants

AI-powered assistants can manage personal tokens, suggest trades or track goals, acting as a digital financial advisor.

Example:

Cleo and **Emma** are traditional AI budgeting apps; similar tools in Web3 can help users allocate their tokens, track expenses and identify opportunities for growth.

c) Risk Management

AI can monitor risks such as token price volatility, liquidity issues or smart contract vulnerabilities, alerting users before problems arise.

Example:

AI-driven tools like **Halborn** audit smart contracts and monitor token liquidity pools to ensure stability and security.

Optimizing Community Tokens with AI

a) Enhancing Governance Efficiency

AI can assist DAOs in processing large volumes of data and offering actionable recommendations for token-based decisions.

Example:

A DAO managing a local community token might use AI to analyze member voting patterns and propose governance changes to improve participation rates.

b) Custom Incentive Structures

AI can tailor incentive programs to community members based on their contributions and behavior.

Example:

A gaming guild DAO could use AI to track player activity and reward top contributors with additional tokens, fostering engagement.

c) Fraud Detection and Prevention

AI algorithms can identify unusual transactions or malicious activity, protecting token ecosystems from fraud.

Example:

AI security tools like **Chainalysis** can monitor token transactions and flag suspicious activities, safeguarding the community's assets.

AI and Personalization in the Metaverse

AI can enhance the integration of personal currencies within the metaverse, tailoring financial experiences to individual preferences.

a) Personalized Virtual Economies

AI can curate experiences and offerings based on users' financial habits and token holdings.

Example:

A personal token holder in a metaverse like **The Sandbox** could receive AI-driven recommendations for exclusive NFTs, events or collaborations that align with their interests.

b) Adaptive Exchange Rates

AI can create dynamic exchange rates for personal tokens based on their utility and demand across different platforms in the metaverse.

Example:

A creator's token could be automatically valued higher on platforms where the creator is more active, ensuring fair exchange rates for users.

Real-World Examples of AI and Blockchain Convergence

a) AI-Driven Trading Bots

Platforms like **3Commas** and **Pionex** leverage AI to automate trading strategies, providing insights that could also apply to managing personal currencies.

b) AI in Token Launch Platforms

Projects like **Balancer** use AI to optimize liquidity pools, demonstrating how similar tools could assist individuals launching personal or community tokens.

c) AI for NFT Valuation

Tools like **Upshot** use AI to appraise NFTs, which could extend to valuing personal tokens in niche markets.

Challenges of Integrating AI with Personal Currencies

a) Data Privacy Concerns

AI relies on data to function effectively, which raises concerns about how user information is collected, stored and used.

b) Algorithm Bias

If AI models are not trained on diverse data, they may make biased decisions, limiting their utility.

c) Accessibility Issues

Advanced AI tools may remain out of reach for individuals in underbanked regions, creating a digital divide.

The Future of AI in Personal Currencies

As AI technology evolves, it will become even more integrated with personal currencies, enabling smarter, more adaptive systems. Future advancements may include:

- AI-powered **reputation scoring** systems for personal tokens.
- Automated community-building tools that use AI to identify and onboard like-minded contributors.

- Predictive governance systems that forecast community needs and propose optimal token allocation strategies.

AI is set to revolutionize the management and optimization of personal currencies, making them more efficient, accessible and impactful. By harnessing AI's predictive and analytical capabilities, users can unlock the full potential of their personal tokens, navigating the complexities of Web3 with ease. As AI and blockchain continue to converge, the future of personalized finance looks smarter, more inclusive and highly adaptable to individual and community needs.

In the next section, we'll explore **ethical considerations in personal currencies**, focusing on data privacy, inclusivity and environmental impact.

Redefining Global Economics

Vision for Decentralized and Community-Driven Financial Systems

The rise of personal currencies and blockchain-powered ecosystems is reshaping the global economic landscape. By decentralizing control over money creation and financial systems, individuals and communities are gaining unprecedented power to create, manage and exchange value on their terms. This shift paves the way for a world where economic activity is not dictated by centralized institutions but by networks of empowered participants.

From Centralized to Decentralized Economies

a) Traditional Centralized Systems

In the current global economy, central banks and governments control the issuance and flow of money. This centralization often leads to inefficiencies, including inflation, wealth inequality and exclusion of the underbanked.

Example:

Hyperinflation in Venezuela has eroded the value of the national currency, forcing many to turn to decentralized cryptocurrencies like Bitcoin as a more stable alternative.

b) Decentralized Economies

In decentralized systems, individuals and communities can issue and manage their own currencies. This allows for localized economic systems that cater to specific needs and priorities.

Example:

The town of Wörgl in Austria introduced a local currency during the Great Depression to stimulate the local economy. Blockchain now enables similar initiatives on a global scale with far greater transparency and security.

Empowering Communities Through Decentralization

a) Community-Driven Financial Systems

Blockchain enables communities to create tokens that reflect their shared values and goals, aligning economic incentives with collective growth.

Example:

Friends With Benefits (FWB): A tokenized social community where members contribute to its growth and governance by holding and using the FWB token.

b) Reducing Dependency on Centralized Institutions

With decentralized finance (DeFi) platforms, communities can create financial services such as lending, borrowing and savings without relying on banks.

Example:

Platforms like **Aave** and **Uniswap** allow users to lend and trade assets directly, bypassing traditional banking systems.

Tokenization and Its Economic Impact

Tokenization allows for fractional ownership and access to assets that were previously illiquid or inaccessible. This democratizes wealth creation and enables new economic models.

a) Tokenizing Real-World Assets

Physical assets like real estate, art and even intellectual property can be tokenized, enabling fractional ownership and global trade.

Example:

RealT, a platform that tokenizes real estate, allows individuals worldwide to invest in U.S. properties through blockchain technology.

b) Tokenized Labor and Skills

Personal currencies enable individuals to tokenize their time, skills or creative output, creating new income streams.

Example:

A freelance developer could issue a personal token that represents hours of their time, which clients can buy and redeem for services.

Redefining Global Trade and Collaboration

a) Borderless Transactions

Blockchain eliminates the need for intermediaries like banks, enabling instant and cost-effective cross-border payments.

Example:

Migrant workers often lose a significant portion of their earnings to remittance fees. Platforms like **Stellar** and **Ripple** use blockchain to facilitate low-cost international transfers, empowering workers to send more money home.

b) Cooperative Economies

Decentralized Autonomous Organizations (DAOs) allow people from across the globe to pool resources and collaborate on shared goals.

Example:

Gitcoin DAO supports open-source projects by pooling funds from contributors worldwide, enabling a more equitable funding model.

A Vision for Decentralized Global Economics

a) Financial Inclusion for All

Decentralized systems can bring billions of unbanked individuals into the global economy by providing them with access to financial tools through smartphones and the internet.

Example:

In Kenya, mobile money services like **M-Pesa** have paved the way for financial inclusion. Blockchain can amplify this by offering decentralized savings and credit systems.

b) Localized Economies with Global Impact

Personal and community currencies enable localized economic systems while remaining connected to the global economy, creating a hybrid model of local empowerment and global integration.

Example:

A rural community could issue a token to fund local infrastructure projects, with the token's value tied to the project's success. Investors worldwide could participate, aligning local development with global investment opportunities.

Challenges in Transitioning to Decentralized Economics

a) Resistance from Traditional Institutions

Governments and banks may resist decentralized systems due to the loss of control over monetary policy and financial infrastructure.

b) Technological Barriers

Adoption of decentralized systems requires robust infrastructure, including internet access and user-friendly blockchain platforms.

c) Volatility and Speculation

Decentralized currencies often face volatility, which can deter widespread adoption for everyday use.

The Future: A Decentralized World Economy

Imagine a world where financial power is distributed among individuals and communities:

- **Personal Financial Freedom:** Individuals can issue and manage their own currencies, enabling them to directly benefit from their productivity and creativity.
- **Community Empowerment:** Communities can pool resources and make collective decisions, creating self-sustaining economies that align with their values.
- **Global Collaboration:** Borderless trade and tokenized assets enable unprecedented collaboration and economic integration, fostering a more equitable global economy.

The vision for decentralized and community-driven financial systems is not just a theoretical possibility - it's already taking shape. By leveraging blockchain technology and personal currencies, we can redefine global economics, shifting power from centralized entities to the individuals and communities that drive real value creation.

Appendices

Empowering the Individual in the Digital Age: A Recap

The journey we've explored together in this book highlights one powerful truth: we are entering an age where individuals have more control over their money, creativity and communities than ever before. The rise of Web3, blockchain and cryptocurrencies offers tools that allow anyone to create, exchange and grow value without needing permission from traditional systems.

We began by looking at the history of money and how centralized systems have controlled wealth for centuries. Then, we saw how blockchain technology has redefined trust by making systems open, transparent and decentralized. Cryptocurrencies started as digital cash but quickly evolved into smart contracts, programmable money and personal tokens - tools that anyone can use to build their own economy.

Web3, often called the "Internet of Value," has shown us how decentralization creates opportunities for creators, communities and businesses. Whether it's an artist launching an NFT, a community creating a DAO or a local economy issuing its own token, the possibilities are endless.

At the same time, we've discussed the challenges - regulations, security risks and the hurdles of mass adoption. These obstacles remind us that new systems require responsibility and innovation to succeed.

Despite these challenges, the future of personal currencies is bright. As tools like Layer 2 solutions, no-code platforms and AI evolve, they will make it even easier for people to access these opportunities. Imagine a world where your currency reflects your unique value, a community's token supports shared goals and everyone participates in a global economy that prioritizes fairness and inclusivity.

This is the power of Web3 and blockchain: to put control back into the hands of individuals. It's a shift from centralized power to personal empowerment, a transformation that allows each of us to dream, create and thrive in ways never before possible.

As we move forward, remember: you don't need to be a tech expert or a financial guru to participate. All you need is a desire to learn, adapt and explore this new frontier. The tools are there. The opportunities are waiting. The future is yours to build.

Let's embrace this digital age together and use it to empower not just ourselves but also the communities and causes we care about most. Your journey starts here. Your currency, your value, your power - it's all in your hands

Glossary of Terms

A

- **Airdrop:** The distribution of free tokens to wallet addresses, often as a promotional strategy or reward for early supporters.
- **Altcoin:** Any cryptocurrency that is not Bitcoin, offering various functionalities and use cases in the blockchain ecosystem.
- **Asset Tokenization:** The process of representing real-world assets like real estate, stocks or commodities as tokens on a blockchain.
- **Automated Market Maker (AMM):** A DeFi protocol that facilitates trading by using algorithms instead of order books (e.g., Uniswap).

B

- **Blockchain:** A distributed, immutable ledger that records transactions in a secure and transparent manner.
- **Blockchain Explorer:** A tool that allows users to search and view blockchain data such as transactions, blocks and wallet addresses.
- **Bridges:** Protocols that connect different blockchain networks, allowing for the transfer of assets and data across them.
- **Burning Tokens:** The process of permanently removing tokens from circulation, often to reduce supply and increase scarcity.

C

- **Centralized Finance (CeFi):** Traditional financial systems and institutions where control is centralized, such as banks and stock exchanges.
- **Cold Wallet:** An offline wallet used to store cryptocurrencies, providing enhanced security against hacking.
- **Consensus Mechanism:** The process by which blockchain networks agree on the validity of transactions (e.g., Proof of Work, Proof of Stake).
- **Cross-Chain Communication:** The ability of different blockchain networks to interact and exchange information or assets.
- **Cryptocurrency:** Digital currency secured by cryptography, often used as a medium of exchange or store of value.

D

- **DAO (Decentralized Autonomous Organization):** An organization governed by smart contracts and token holders, without centralized leadership.
- **DApp (Decentralized Application):** An application built on blockchain technology that operates without central control.
- **Decentralization:** The distribution of control and decision-making away from a central authority.
- **Decentralized Finance (DeFi):** Financial applications built on blockchain that operate without intermediaries.
- **Digital Identity:** A blockchain-based identity that is verifiable, secure and can be used across various platforms and applications.

E

- **EIP (Ethereum Improvement Proposal):** A design document proposing changes to the Ethereum network, such as upgrades or new features.
- **ERC Standards:** Technical standards for tokens on the Ethereum blockchain (e.g., ERC-20 for fungible tokens, ERC-721 for NFTs).
- **Ethereum:** A blockchain platform known for its ability to deploy smart contracts and decentralized applications (dApps).

F

- **Fiat Currency:** Government-issued money that is not backed by a physical commodity, such as the US Dollar or Euro.
- **Fractional Ownership:** The concept of owning a portion of an asset, often facilitated by tokenization.
- **Fork:** A change to a blockchain protocol that creates a new version, such as a hard fork (e.g., Bitcoin Cash) or soft fork.
- **Fungible:** Assets or tokens that are interchangeable with one another, like Bitcoin or fiat currency.

G

- **Gas Fees:** Transaction fees paid to miners or validators to process and validate operations on a blockchain.
- **Genesis Block:** The first block ever created in a blockchain, forming the foundation of the ledger.
- **Governance Token:** A type of token that allows holders to participate in decision-making processes within a blockchain project or DAO.

H

- **Hard Fork:** A permanent divergence from the previous blockchain protocol, resulting in a new chain (e.g., Ethereum and Ethereum Classic).
- **Hash Function:** A cryptographic algorithm that converts data into a fixed-length string, used to secure blockchain transactions.
- **HODL:** A popular term in the cryptocurrency community meaning to hold onto assets rather than sell, derived from a misspelling of "hold."

I

- **ICO (Initial Coin Offering):** A fundraising method where new cryptocurrencies or tokens are sold to investors before launching.
- **Interchain Communication:** The exchange of information or transactions between different blockchain ecosystems.
- **Interoperability:** The ability of different blockchain networks to communicate and operate with each other seamlessly.
- **Immutable:** The characteristic of blockchain that ensures data, once recorded, cannot be altered or deleted.

L

- **Layer 2 Solutions:** Secondary protocols built on top of a blockchain to improve scalability and reduce transaction costs (e.g., Polygon, Optimism).
- **Liquidity Mining:** Earning rewards by providing liquidity to DeFi platforms or liquidity pools.
- **Liquidity Pool:** A collection of funds locked in a smart contract used to facilitate decentralized trading and lending.

- **Lightning Network:** A Layer 2 solution designed to improve Bitcoin's scalability by enabling faster and cheaper transactions.

M

- **Mainnet:** The live version of a blockchain network where real transactions occur, as opposed to testnets used for development.
- **Market Cap:** The total value of a cryptocurrency, calculated by multiplying the token price by its circulating supply.
- **Metaverse:** A digital universe combining virtual reality, blockchain and social interactions, often incorporating personal and community currencies.
- **Mining:** The process of validating blockchain transactions and adding them to the ledger, typically rewarded with cryptocurrency.

N

- **NFT (Non-Fungible Token):** A unique digital asset representing ownership of specific items like art, music or collectibles on the blockchain.
- **Node:** A computer that participates in a blockchain network by validating and storing transaction data.
- **Nonce:** A number used only once in cryptographic communication, often seen in Proof of Work mining.

O

- **On-Chain Governance:** A decision-making process conducted directly on the blockchain, typically using governance tokens.
- **Oracles:** Services that provide blockchain systems with external data (e.g., weather data or stock prices).

P

- **Permissionless Blockchain:** A blockchain where anyone can join, participate and validate transactions, like Bitcoin or Ethereum.
- **Private Key:** A secret code that allows users to access and manage their blockchain assets.
- **Proof of Stake (PoS):** A consensus mechanism where validators are chosen based on the number of tokens they hold and are willing to "stake."
- **Proof of Work (PoW):** A consensus mechanism requiring miners to solve complex mathematical problems to validate transactions.
- **Public Key:** A cryptographic code shared with others to receive cryptocurrency, paired with a private key for security.

R

- **Rollups:** A Layer 2 solution that bundles multiple transactions into a single batch to improve scalability and reduce fees.
- **Rug Pull:** A type of scam in which developers abandon a project and take investors' funds.

S

- **Satoshi:** The smallest unit of Bitcoin, named after its creator, Satoshi Nakamoto (1 BTC = 100,000,000 satoshis).
- **Smart Contract:** Self-executing code on a blockchain that enforces agreements without the need for intermediaries.
- **Smart Contract Auditing:** The process of reviewing and verifying smart contract code to ensure security and functionality.

- **Stablecoin:** A cryptocurrency pegged to a stable asset, such as the US Dollar, to minimize price volatility.

T

- **Tokenization:** The process of converting assets or rights into digital tokens on a blockchain.
- **Tokenomics:** The study and design of the economic model and value system of a cryptocurrency or token.
- **Token Burn:** The process of intentionally destroying tokens to reduce supply, often to increase the token's value.
- **Token Standard:** A set of rules a token must follow to operate within a specific blockchain ecosystem.

U

- **Universal Basic Income (UBI):** A concept where blockchain-based programs distribute income universally, often through social tokens or DAOs.
- **Unpermissioned Blockchain:** A network that does not require prior approval to join, allowing open participation.
- **Utility Token:** A token that provides access to a product or service within a specific blockchain ecosystem.

V

- **Validator:** A participant in a Proof of Stake blockchain who validates transactions and earns rewards by staking tokens.
- **Virtual Machine:** Software that runs on blockchains (e.g., Ethereum Virtual Machine) to execute smart contracts.

- **Volatility:** The degree of price fluctuation in a cryptocurrency, which can affect its adoption and utility.

W

- **Wallet:** A digital tool used to store, send and receive cryptocurrencies and tokens securely.
- **Warm Wallet:** A cryptocurrency wallet connected to the internet, often used for frequent transactions but less secure than cold wallets.
- **Web3:** The next generation of the internet, emphasizing decentralization, user ownership and the integration of blockchain technologies.
- **Wrapped Token:** A token that represents another cryptocurrency on a different blockchain, enabling interoperability (e.g., Wrapped Bitcoin on Ethereum).

Y

- **Yield Farming:** The practice of earning rewards by staking or lending cryptocurrency in DeFi protocols.

Z

- **Zero-Knowledge Proof:** A cryptographic method allowing one party to prove they know something without revealing the actual information.
- **ZK-Rollups:** A Layer 2 scaling solution that uses zero-knowledge proofs to bundle transactions efficiently.

Resources for Learning Blockchain and Web3

If you're excited to learn more about blockchain, cryptocurrencies and Web3, here's a list of resources to help you on your journey. These include beginner-friendly materials, technical deep dives and platforms for hands-on practice.

Beginner-Friendly Resources

1. **Websites and Blogs:**
   - CoinDesk: News and insights on blockchain and cryptocurrency trends.
   - Cointelegraph: A leading source for crypto-related news and educational articles.
   - Ethereum.org Learn: Beginner guides to blockchain, smart contracts and decentralized applications (dApps).
2. **YouTube Channels:**
   - **Andreas M. Antonopoulos:** Simplifies complex blockchain concepts with real-world examples.
   - **Whiteboard Crypto:** Breaks down blockchain topics in simple terms using visual explanations.
   - **Finematics:** Focuses on DeFi and blockchain technologies, explained in a concise, engaging manner.
3. **Books:**
   - "The Basics of Bitcoins and Blockchains" by Antony Lewis: A beginner's guide to blockchain technology.
   - "Mastering Bitcoin" by Andreas M. Antonopoulos: A deeper dive into Bitcoin and its technical aspects.

- *"Mastering Ethereum"* by Andreas M. Antonopoulos and Gavin Wood: An essential guide to Ethereum and smart contracts.

4. **Podcasts:**
   - **Unchained:** Hosted by Laura Shin, covering blockchain news and expert interviews.
   - **The Pomp Podcast:** Focuses on Bitcoin, blockchain and business.
   - **Bankless:** Offers insights into DeFi, Ethereum and how to go "bankless" with Web3 tools.

Intermediate to Advanced Learning

1. **Online Courses:**
   - **Coursera:**
     - *"Blockchain Basics"* by the University at Buffalo.
     - *"Decentralized Finance (DeFi)"* by Duke University.
   - **edX:**
     - *"Blockchain for Business"* by the Linux Foundation.
   - **Udemy:**
     - *"Ethereum and Solidity: The Complete Developer's Guide"* by Stephen Grider.
2. **Developer-Focused Resources:**
   - **Solidity Documentation:** soliditylang.org: Learn how to write smart contracts.
   - **Remix IDE:** An online tool to practice coding smart contracts in Solidity.
   - **Hardhat:** A development environment for building on Ethereum.

- **GitHub Repositories:** Explore open-source blockchain projects to learn from real-world examples.
3. **Blockchain Academies and Bootcamps:**
    - **Blockchain Council:** Offers certifications and courses for blockchain developers and enthusiasts.
    - **Alchemy University:** Provides free and premium Web3 development courses.
    - **Consensys Academy:** Ethereum-focused training programs.

Hands-On Learning Platforms

1. **Testnets and Faucets:**
    - **Rinkeby, Goerli and Mumbai Testnets:** Practice deploying smart contracts and interacting with blockchains without spending real money.
    - **Faucets:** Obtain free test tokens to use on testnets (e.g., Alchemy Faucet).
2. **Play-to-Learn Platforms:**
    - **CryptoZombies:** Teaches Solidity by building a simple blockchain-based game.
    - **Ethernaut:** A Web3 security-focused game to learn about smart contracts and vulnerabilities.
3. **DAO Memberships and Hackathons:**
    - **Gitcoin:** Participate in blockchain hackathons and earn rewards.
    - **Kernel:** A Web3 learning community offering deep discussions and mentorship.

Communities and Forums

1. **Reddit Communities:**
   - r/cryptocurrency: General discussions about blockchain and crypto.
   - r/ethdev: Ethereum development-focused community.
   - r/defi: Dedicated to decentralized finance topics.
2. **Discord Servers:**
   - Join project-specific servers like Ethereum, Solana or Avalanche for discussions and updates.
   - Participate in DAO communities for hands-on involvement in governance and project development.
3. **Meetups and Events:**
   - **Blockchain Meetup Groups:** Check Meetup.com for local blockchain and Web3 events.
   - **Web3 Conferences:** Attend events like ETHGlobal, Consensus or Devcon for networking and learning.

News Aggregators and Tools

1. **News Aggregators:**
   - **CryptoPanic:** Aggregates news from various crypto sources and social media.
   - **Messari:** Offers research and insights into blockchain projects.
2. **Tracking Tools:**
   - **CoinMarketCap:** Tracks cryptocurrency prices, market caps and rankings.

- **Etherscan:** A blockchain explorer for Ethereum.

These resources provide a mix of theoretical knowledge and practical experience to help you dive into the blockchain and Web3 space. Whether you're a beginner or an advanced learner, there's something here to empower you on your journey.

Guide to Token Launch Tools and Platforms

Launching a token in the Web3 ecosystem has become increasingly accessible thanks to a variety of tools and platforms. Here's a guide to the most popular tools and platforms categorized by complexity, functionality and ease of use.

No-Code Tools for Beginners

For individuals or small teams without programming skills, these no-code tools simplify token creation:

a. CoinTool

- **Features:**
    - Create custom tokens on Ethereum, Binance Smart Chain (BSC), Polygon and other networks.
    - Supports standard token types like ERC-20 and BEP-20.
    - Intuitive interface for beginners.
- **Use Case:** Best for simple token launches without requiring smart contract coding.
- **Website:** cointool.app

b. Mintable

- **Features:**
    - Create NFTs and utility tokens with no coding required.
    - Focuses on NFTs but also allows general token launches.

- **Use Case:** Ideal for artists or creators looking to tokenize their work.
- **Website:** mintable.app

c. TokenMint by Horizen

- **Features:**
    - Drag-and-drop interface for launching tokens.
    - Supports basic customizations like supply and distribution.
- **Use Case:** Simple community token launches with limited technical setup.
- **Website:** tokenmint.io

Developer-Friendly Platforms

For users with technical expertise or developer support, these platforms offer more flexibility:

a. Ethereum (ERC-20)

- **Features:**
    - The most widely used blockchain for token creation.
    - Smart contracts written in Solidity.
    - Massive ecosystem of tools, wallets and dApps.
- **Use Case:** Suitable for creating tokens with advanced functionalities like governance, staking or DeFi.
- **Website:** ethereum.org

b. Binance Smart Chain (BEP-20)

- **Features:**

- Cheaper and faster than Ethereum, with similar functionality.
- Supports the BEP-20 token standard.
- **Use Case:** Ideal for projects that need low transaction fees and fast confirmations.
- **Website:** bscscan.com

c. Solana

- **Features:**
  - High-speed blockchain with low fees.
  - Supports SPL token standard.
- **Use Case:** Perfect for scalable applications like gaming and NFTs.
- **Website:** solana.com

d. Polygon

- **Features:**
  - Ethereum Layer 2 scaling solution.
  - Supports ERC-20 tokens with lower fees.
- **Use Case:** Ideal for projects that want Ethereum compatibility without high costs.
- **Website:** polygon.technology

Smart Contract Tools

For advanced users, these tools help create and deploy customized smart contracts:

a. OpenZeppelin

- **Features:**
  - Pre-audited smart contract templates.

- o Includes ERC-20, ERC-721 and ERC-1155 standards.
- o Built-in security features to prevent vulnerabilities.
- **Use Case:** Developers seeking reliable, customizable contracts.
- **Website:** openzeppelin.com

b. Hardhat

- **Features:**
  - o Development framework for Ethereum-based projects.
  - o Allows for local testing and debugging of smart contracts.
- **Use Case:** Developers building complex token ecosystems.
- **Website:** hardhat.org

c. Remix IDE

- **Features:**
  - o Browser-based IDE for coding and deploying smart contracts.
  - o Ideal for Solidity programming beginners.
- **Use Case:** Small-scale projects or testing new contract ideas.
- **Website:** remix.ethereum.org

Platforms for Initial Token Offerings (ITOs/ICOs)

For projects planning token launches with public fundraising, these platforms provide ready-to-use tools:

a. Polkastarter

- **Features:**
    - Decentralized launchpad for Initial DEX Offerings (IDOs).
    - Built-in token sale and distribution features.
- **Use Case:** Fundraising for blockchain startups.
- **Website:** polkastarter.com

b. Bounce Finance

- **Features:**
    - Token auction and sale platform.
    - Supports Dutch, sealed-bid and fixed-price auctions.
- **Use Case:** Flexible fundraising for token projects.
- **Website:** bounce.finance

c. CoinList

- **Features:**
    - Centralized platform for token sales and staking.
    - Handles compliance and KYC processes.
- **Use Case:** Large-scale token launches targeting global audiences.
- **Website:** coinlist.co

Security and Auditing Tools

Securing your token's smart contract is critical. These tools help ensure your token is safe for users:

a. CertiK

- **Features:**
    - Smart contract auditing services.

- o Security assessments for blockchain projects.
- **Use Case:** Projects launching tokens and dApps that need security guarantees.
- **Website:** certik.com

b. Quantstamp

- **Features:**
  - o Automated and manual smart contract audits.
  - o Bug detection and security fixes.
- **Use Case:** High-stakes projects requiring robust audits.
- **Website:** quantstamp.com

Token Management and Analytics

After launching a token, these tools help manage and monitor your project:

a. Etherscan and BscScan

- **Features:**
  - o Blockchain explorers to track token transactions and holder data.
  - o Useful for transparency and community engagement.
- **Use Case:** Monitoring token performance and distribution.
- **Websites:** etherscan.io, bscscan.com

b. CoinGecko and CoinMarketCap

- **Features:**

- - Token listing platforms for price tracking and market data.
  - Gain visibility for your token.
- **Use Case:** Promoting your token to a wider audience.
- **Websites:** coingecko.com, coinmarketcap.com

Tips for Choosing the Right Tool

1. **Define Your Goals:** Determine whether your token is for fundraising, governance, utility or community building.
2. **Consider the Network:** Choose a blockchain based on transaction fees, speed and user base.
3. **Test Thoroughly:** Use testnets and auditing tools to identify and fix issues before launch.
4. **Stay Compliant:** Be aware of local and global regulations to avoid legal complications.

With these tools and platforms, launching your own token is easier than ever. Choose the one that fits your project's goals and start building your Web3 journey!

www.ingramcontent.com/pod-product-compliance
Lightning Source LLC
Chambersburg PA
CBHW071023240526
45469CB00006BD/2055